# BAILOUT RICHES!

# BAILOUT RICHES!

How Everyday Investors Can

*Make a Fortune*

Buying Bad Loans for

*Pennies on the Dollar*

# BILL BARTMANN

## WITH JONATHAN ROZEK

WILEY

John Wiley & Sons, Inc.

ISBN: 978-0-470-47825-7

Printed in the United States of America.

10 9 8 7 6 5 4 3 2 1

# CONTENTS

CHAPTER

1

# I've Seen This Movie Before, and Know How It Ends: I Make a Billion Dollars

I've bought a few thousand books over the years, so I know the
process you're going through. You've checked out the front and
back covers, and now want to know: Is this book for real, or is
this just another writer hoping to make the Big Time by impressing
you with a theory?

Let me save you some time and give you the guts of this book,
condensed to the most extreme level. Here goes:

1. Most people think the multi-trillion-dollar U.S. government
   bailout is a new situation without equal in history. The truth is
   that a similar event occurred in the 1980s, though on a smaller
   scale.

2. The last time it happened, I went from being bankrupt to a self-made billionaire by investing in assets the government was liquidating. I used none of my own money—because I had no money.

3. This time around, the opportunity is even bigger. I'm going to ride it one more time. This book will show you how to ride your own way to enormous wealth.

There you have it. That's the whole book. If the preceding three paragraphs do not interest you, then I suggest you save your time and put this book down. Go check out a "how to get rich quick" book by yet another author who wants to become famous and really wealthy, but in reality is neither. Have a nice life.

What? You're still reading? In that case, you deserve a little more explanation of who I am, and why I am qualified to write this book.

- *Inc.* magazine featured me on the cover as "The Billionaire Nobody Knows."
- My annual after-tax take-home pay in some years exceeded $100 million.
- I was ranked as the 25th-wealthiest person in America, according to one magazine.
- I paid cash for my own Gulfstream IV jet, and my private security detail consisted of former Secret Service agents from the presidential detail.

I could go on, but you get the idea.

You may be thinking: "Bartmann. Bartmann. Where have I heard that name before? Was this guy one of those rich kids whose daddy handed him the keys to a Ferrari? Was he born with a silver spoon in his mouth?"

That would not describe my upbringing. In fact, you know the baseball saying, "Three strikes and you're out"? I was raised with about 15 strikes already against me:

- I was born next to a pig slaughterhouse.
- My dad was a janitor and my mom cleaned houses.
- We were evicted from two places when I was growing up, because they were declared "unfit for human habitation."
- I grew up with a pet dog—not to be my buddy, but to keep the rats off me as I slept at night.
- I lived for months at a time under a bridge viaduct and in a hayloft, and routinely ate out of Dumpsters.
- I was a gang member and an alcoholic by the age of 17.
- One night, in a drunken stupor, I fell down a flight of stairs and shattered part of my spine. I was told I would never walk again.

I could go on about my sordid past, but you get the idea.

I bring all of this up so you understand that I am not a distinguished professor who's cooked up a great new theory. They're a dime a dozen at the bookstore.

I'm also not a guy who made it big sometime in the past, but under entirely different circumstances than we face today. Those people are fine subjects for history lessons, but not for getting current, profitable information.

I'll tell you exactly where I was when I decided to write this book: I was on my exercise bike in late 2008, watching the news about the $700 billion government bailout bill that had just passed.

The assistant secretary of the treasury had called a press conference, and was explaining the outlines of the rescue plan the government was unveiling. He said it was a seven-step plan.

By the third step, I could recite out loud each step before he did.

How could I possibly know what the assistant secretary was going to say before he said it?

Because I had seen this movie before, and I knew the ending. The asset disposition plan that the government was unfolding was the same plan it used in the last crisis. It worked fine once before, so they decided to dust it off and use it again.

Please stop for a moment and consider the essence of what I just explained to you:

I made a billion dollars from a standing start (okay, that's not exactly true; I was a million bucks in the hole). I did it without having the benefit of anyone showing me the ropes.

You, on the other hand, are in a much better position right now. An even bigger opportunity is presenting itself, and you have me as your guide.

## What Opportunity Am I Talking About?

With one stimulus plan after another, the government is in the process of buying up banks with hundreds of billions of dollars of troubled assets. As you've heard everyone stress, the government wants to get back its couple trillion just as quickly as possible.

That means those banks will soon be dumping unheard-of amounts of assets onto the market at great discounts.

If you know what you're doing (which you will), and know where to look (which you will), you can buy bundles of these opportunities with 100 percent financing. Then you can manage the assets in such a way as to create a steady stream of cold, hard, immediate cash coming to you.

Is it beginning to dawn on you that the few bucks you just spent on this book might be the best investment of your life?

In the following chapters, I describe each aspect of this opportunity in much greater detail. You will see how the whole picture fits together. You'll have a whirlwind exposure to interesting but little-known parts of the world of finance.

The best part is you'll close this book with a clear idea of the next steps you can take to make a fortune of your own.

It's time for the very first question I know is on your mind. Throughout this book, I'll stop to answer the questions that alert readers should be asking themselves. Here's the first one:

"Bill, if this is such a good opportunity, why would you possibly share it with the world? Why wouldn't you just keep it to yourself?"

The answer is simple: There's plenty of money out there for both of us.

Even when I made my first billion, I was only dipping a spoon into the ocean of dough I saw before me. Years ago I passed the point where I thought that a dollar in someone else's pocket was one less dollar in mine.

That's poverty thinking. Instead, when you've made a lot of money, you begin to see opportunity everywhere.

Trust me: I'm fully capitalizing on the current situation. But even I cannot get my arms around the entire opportunity, all for myself!

## How This Book Is Organized

There are specific steps for us to cover in your journey to great wealth. There's nothing magical about any one of them.

The real magic is in applying all of them fairly quickly, while the window of opportunity is still open. You will see in Chapter 2 that this opportunity is indeed temporary. For very practical reasons, this is not something you'll be able to teach your kids to do.

You should also know that you cannot take shortcuts with my system and still get maximum value out of it. You must apply the steps in order.

I'm a fanatic about creating systems. In fact, the Smithsonian Institution has a permanent display featuring some of the financial technology I pioneered. The Harvard Business School taught a case study on my methods.

Therefore, you can be sure that I followed the advice of Albert Einstein, who said: "Things should be made as simple as possible, but no simpler."

Here are the steps I cover in later chapters.

### Realize the Opportunity

Everyone is *looking at* the same stuff coming out of Washington, but only a few people are *seeing* what it means. What really matters is how you interpret the information. I dissect the current bailout in terms of the very specific forces at work that make this such an astonishing opportunity.

### Understand How You Can Take Advantage of It, Regardless of Your Circumstances

There may be a few people who realize the wealth-building potential before us, but many of them will never become wealthy from it. They'll fall into the trap of thinking "My situation is different."

What a pity. They don't realize that we all have different situations. We all have disadvantages, shortcomings, and unfair circumstances of one type or another. Some people like me have had generous helpings of each type of problem. Those are not reasons for failure—they're merely excuses for failure.

It's my job to show you how you can succeed despite having a long list of disadvantages, and I do just that in this section.

### Get Prepared

No, you can't read my book, close the cover, and go to the bank with a fat check. You'll actually have to get off your duff and implement my system. But you will see in this section that it's merely a matter of taking one reasonable step after another. No giant leaps necessary.

### Contact Suppliers of Bad Debt

The network news only talks about "failed mortgages" that banks are holding. Yes, they have a lot of those, but there's a whole rainbow of other asset opportunities for you to work with. I describe the nature and differences of these opportunities, and whom to contact so you can participate.

## Analyze Opportunities

Your judgment is never better than your information. If you do not know what to make of a great opportunity, you can hardly take advantage of it. You must have a tested and proven method to analyze many deals quickly, and find the ones that are worth pursuing.

Even in this special period with excellent opportunities, there will be a lot of garbage to contend with. After all, even if you are the owner of the world's richest deposits of gold or diamonds, you must swiftly sort through mountains of worthless rock in order to find those precious glimmers of value. It's no different with investment opportunities. Fortunately for you, I am your guide.

## Land Your First Deal

Staring at a wonderful opportunity will do you no good. You must act on it. As a new investor in these sorts of things, you may find it scary to leave the world of analysis and take action.

It need not be scary if you know what you're doing and are not taking a big risk. When I developed my systems, I had nothing with which to risk. I could only take advantage of opportunities that didn't require much time or any money to nail down. I show you how to do the same.

## Manage Your Deal

You lock in your profit when you invest in an opportunity, but you turn that profit potential into actual dollars only by managing it.

Before you start thinking "I don't have time to brush my teeth, let alone manage some exotic asset," hang on: I'll show you that you don't have to touch a thing if you don't want to. There are asset managers available who do this sort of work for a living.

## Wrap Up Your Deal

After you have maximized the value of your deal, it's time to move on. I explain the exit strategies open to you, and when to choose which. You'll have the luxury of deciding whether you want to continue to get a stream of income from these assets, or settle for a lump sum when you sell them to others. It's a nice problem to have.

## Reward Yourself

I'm a big believer in hard work, but I don't believe in doing so merely for the sake of hard work. It needs to result in rewards, and that's the purpose of this book: to show you the path to exceedingly large rewards.

Even though I could buy pretty much any toy at any price on planet Earth, one of the greatest treasures I have is a little wooden elephant that cost pennies.

Mother Teresa gave it to me. If you don't already realize this, you'll soon know that helping others in need is one of the most rewarding uses of your new fortune. After I took care of my loved ones' needs, I found that donating to charity made me feel wonderful. We'll talk more about all the pleasant choices you'll have once you get your money machine humming.

## Get Better to Grow Larger

Trust me: Once you complete one cycle of this money-making process, you'll lie awake at night, wanting the alarm clock to ring so you can bound out of bed and grow your empire even bigger.

I know a thing or two about growing businesses: My company was listed in *Inc.* magazine's "500 Fastest-Growing Companies" for four years in a row. In fact, the only other company on that list to ever grow as fast, as quickly as we did, was Microsoft.

I'll be your guide to growing your endeavor as quickly and as large as you wish.

## In the Next Chapter

You are about to get a real eye-opener: In the next chapter, I lay out why the opportunity before us is truly a once-in-a-lifetime event. It's a perfect storm of ways to profit, all coming together very quickly.

Most giant storms come and go so fast that many people never know what hit them. You're different: You are reading this book and will be prepared to benefit like very few can.

# Realize the Opportunity

January 24, 1848, started out as a pretty average day, but it didn't end that way. On that day, James Marshall discovered gold at Sutter's Mill in Coloma, California.

It wasn't that Marshall changed his standard of living between breakfast and dinner. The only thing that changed is that he very quickly and profoundly realized the opportunity that lay at his feet.

James Marshall was fortunate in two respects: He was exposed to great opportunity, and he immediately recognized it.

When I made a billion dollars, I was also exposed to great opportunity, but I did not recognize it right away. In fact, when I first saw that opportunity, I distinctly remember thinking to myself: "Only an idiot would do that!"

Let me tell you the brief story of what it looks like when a billion-dollar opportunity knocks at your door.

As I told you in the first chapter, I did not have your typical Beaver Cleaver upbringing. I didn't get good at baseball, riding a bike, or fishing with my dad. Instead, I got good at drinking a case of beer at night, picking fights with rival gang members, and fishing food out of Dumpsters.

I'll write an autobiography sometime so you can get the whole, colorful picture of my background. Suffice it to say that in 1986, I had straightened myself out and was running a successful oil drilling pipe supply company—until the bottom fell out of the oil business. The price of oil went from $40 to $14 in pretty much the space of one week.

It was worse than being just broke. I personally owed a million dollars to the bank that had financed my business. After a while, there was no hope of salvaging that business, so I closed the doors and let all 70 employees go. Kathy, my wife, was making plans to move back to her parents' house with our two young daughters. We weren't digging through the sofa cushions for money, because we had no sofa to dig through.

One day I saw an ad in the *Tulsa World*: It offered a bundle of bad loans (consumer debt) for sale by the government. I thought to myself "What kind of fool would throw good money after bad by buying consumer debt that even collection agencies couldn't collect on!" and I threw away the paper.

The next day I saw that same ad. This time I still thought it was crazy, but I spent a bit longer reading the whole ad.

Then on the third day I saw that ad again. It made me stop and think "Hmm."

That was the billion-dollar opportunity.

To say that it was a long shot is a grotesque understatement. Let me count the ways:

- I did not know a thing about buying consumer loans.
- I had no clue about how to analyze this investment to see if it made any sense.
- I had no money with which to invest in that opportunity, if it did make sense.
- I was in debt to the tune of $1 million, so my own credit was nonexistent.

- I had no office.
- I had no staff.
- There was no one I could turn to for help on this opportunity, because—I later found this out—it was the first of its kind ever to be advertised in the paper.

Other than that, it looked like an interesting deal!
I did have two things going for me, though:

1. I was desperate. This was not an idle hobby I was hoping to pursue. My family needed food, and needed it fast.
2. I had the right mentality. With all the challenges I just listed, it would have been easy for me to say, "There's absolutely no way this can be a good opportunity for me. Not only can I not afford whatever they're offering in the paper, but I wouldn't know what to do with it even if I had it."

That last statement would be logical and sensible for any educated person to make. Yet I did not do that. Instead, the true billion-dollar moment came when I gave myself the momentary permission to think:

- *What if* I could figure out what these assets were all about?
- *What if* they were available not just to big, legitimate companies to buy, but also to little, broke people like me?
- *What if* I could find a way to get this opportunity financed with someone else's money, because I sure don't have any of my own?
- *What if* I could succeed in collecting on some of those loans where the banks and collection agencies failed?

That was a lot of "what if" questions in anyone's book. Yet in that Golden Moment when I asked those questions, I had the willingness to suspend judgment until I got more answers.

Please understand that I was not kidding myself, like some Pollyanna. I had just been through the quick destruction of my livelihood—the pipe company. I was being sued by creditors. Things were not looking good. In fact, I was more than casually contemplating that suicide might be the answer, if only I could make it look like an accident so Kathy could collect on the insurance.

I guess you could say that I was down to my last valuable asset, which was the ability to not look for reasons why something *would not* work (I had plenty of those), but instead to consider why something *might* work.

The next step was to pick up the phone. I shrugged and dialed the number. A man answered the phone. He said that I could "inspect the loan package" (whatever that meant) by coming to their bank office in Tulsa.

I was too broke to take the toll road from Muskogee, Oklahoma, to Tulsa, so I took the long, back roads.

When I arrived in Tulsa, the man showed me to a storage room and plopped a box of files in front of me. He then left me alone and walked out.

I thought to myself: "Great, Bill, you're broke, sitting in Tulsa, looking at a bunch of files you know nothing about. Now what?"

I started to leaf through the files. Each one was banker's shorthand for someone's misfortune: Took out the loan on this date for this much money; made a few payments; defaulted on the loan on this date. Then were numerous notations of all the attempts people had made to collect on the loan.

## How Loans Become Bad Debts, from the Lender's Point of View

It's important for me to explain to you a process I later came to understand.

Let's say Joe Smith takes out a loan for $10,000 at First National Bank. He's buying that bass boat he always wanted, and the loan is "secured" by the boat. The bank can take the boat if Joe doesn't make his payments.

Joe makes the payments for a while, but then life gets in the way. They downsize Joe out of his job, and he falls behind on the bass boat payments.

After that first missed payment date, the loan becomes delinquent. Initially the bank makes nice reminder calls and sends notes. Then the notices become not so nice, and more urgent.

That loan goes 30 days delinquent, and then 60 days. When it starts to head for 90 to 120 days delinquent, the first and most effective thing the bank can and almost always does do is to repossess that collateral.

They grab Joe's boat, and sell it for $4,000. Joe originally owed $10,000, and only made payments totaling $2,000 before getting laid off. Therefore, his balance was $10,000 minus the $2,000 he paid, or $8,000. The bank could only get $4,000 for his dinged-up boat, so Joe is now the proud owner not of a bass boat, but of a "deficiency balance" of $8,000 minus $4,000, or $4,000. The bank still wants its four grand, not counting additional costs it has incurred to try to collect on Joe's loan.

That secured, collateralized loan to Joe for a boat just became an unsecured, uncollateralized loan because the collateral is gone. What I was staring at in the file room in Tulsa was a big pile of uncollateralized, unsecured deficiency balances from lots of borrowers.

It gets better. If Joe continues not to send in payments, then banking rules take over. According to the bank's *charter* or requirements, it has somewhere between 90 and 120 days to collect on that entire loan balance after the date of the last scheduled payment. The interval varies by bank.

At the end of that period, the bank must "charge off" the loan. That means from an accounting perspective the bank must show that loan on its books as having zero value.

Joe still owes the money, but the bank cannot show the loan as an asset any longer. It's "marked to market," and the market value is zero for a loan that's not paying.

Why do they do that? The Federal Deposit Insurance Corporation requires that they do it. The FDIC is the federal entity in charge of maintaining our banking system. It insists on that sort of a rule within the banking industry to make sure that banks are being honest. They don't want banks pretending to show value in loans that have fallen way behind on payments. And so they've put an arbitrary line of demarcation out there, called the *charge-off line*.

Back to Joe's boat. The bank personnel have tried every which way to get Joe to pay that remaining $4,000 on the boat loan. If they are unsuccessful, they'll farm the loan out to a collection agency.

The banking industry uses a terminology of *primary*, *secondary*, and *tertiary* as it relates to the status of accounts that have been sent to a third party for collection. The bank sends Joe's loan—along with other loans in a similar situation—to the collection agency. They're usually given a mandate of "You have 90 (or 120 or 180) days—do the best you can, and we will pay you a commission on the dollars you collect for us."

The collection agency keeps the loans for that period of time, at the end of which the collection agency returns any loans it didn't collect. It's kind of like a consignment clothing store. You put your stuff in—if it sells you get paid, if it doesn't sell, you get your stuff back.

When the loans are returned to the bank after having made this voyage to the first collector, the bank sends them to a second collector. That company takes another whack at collecting on the loans. With its new personnel, new attitude, and different style, it may be effective where prior efforts weren't.

After the second collector takes his turn, he sends back what still is uncollectible. The bank repackages those loans and sends them to the third, tertiary, collector.

What I was staring at in Tulsa had gone delinquent, then was pursued unsuccessfully by the bank after the loans went into the charge-off category. Then these loans had been sent to the first collection agency (the "primary cycle"), which had no success and sent them back to the bank. The loans then went to a second independent agency, which also was unable to collect. The loans went back to the bank and were sent to the third agency, which was as unsuccessful as everyone else at begging, cajoling, and threatening Joe and the other lenders to pay up.

In short, I was staring at the toxic waste of the lending business. Uncollateralized, unsecured loans that had resisted dozens of phone calls and letters by professionals, asking and then demanding to pay up.

Looking at the files, I could see the paper trail that documented these sad tales. I thought to myself what any sane person in my position would think: "What in hell am I thinking? What am I doing here? Why am I looking at this stuff? What could I do with these loans that all the professionals could not do?"

I continued to depress myself: "Why am I wasting my time doing something that I'm absolutely unqualified to do?" I had taken out a few loans in my life, but I'd never tried to collect on one. That ad in the paper was an offering for anyone to bid on this package of toxic-waste loans. If you were successful, you would own the right to collect and keep any dollars you could extract from those borrowers. Um, Hooray.

Because I was so desperate, and because I had made the trip all the way to Tulsa and had no brighter prospects for doing anything else with my life, I shrugged and pulled out my pad and pencil.

This was my logic: "Maybe I could try to formulate an opinion of value—an accurate opinion of value—even if it's a nickel on the dollar or a dime on the dollar. Then mathematically as I average all of the scores for all of the accounts, could I borrow a fraction of that number from *someone* in order to make a bid? And gee, would the bid even be successful?"

I further reasoned that maybe I could luck out and win because it was a sealed bid auction. It isn't like I would have to show up in some big room in front of a guy with a gavel. I could instead formulate an opinion of value, seal it in an envelope, and mail it to these people.

I started with the first file and wrote down the borrower's name and other key facts about the loan. I simply used common sense about what I thought was important about the case. I noted why I thought I could or could not collect on that loan. After looking at

5 and then 25 and then 100 of these loans, I started to get a sense of the "moving parts" in the loan.

I gave each loan an overall number. It was a SWAG.

You don't know what a SWAG is? Well, a "WAG" is a "Wild-Ass Guess." A SWAG is a "Scientific Wild-Ass Guess." It was what I thought I could collect, based on these facts, and in spite of these other facts, because it was a pro-and-con kind of analysis.

I spent days going through these files, because I didn't know you could do it faster. I later learned how to do it one heck of a lot more efficiently. But when I opened that first box of loans and pulled out that first file, I didn't know what I was supposed to see, nor did I know what I was supposed to do with what I saw. And God knows I didn't know all the stuff I *didn't* see.

When I finished going through all of the loans I had a score for each of them, although some of the scores were zero. In fact, many of the scores were zero. I guessed that I couldn't collect anything from those people: Either they had already filed bankruptcy, they were dead, or nobody had been able to reach them by telephone in the last three years. In such situations, what made me think I was going to find them?

I then gathered all my papers and added up all the scores. Overall I thought I could collect six to seven cents on the dollar. But keep in mind that I knew full well that I was only guessing. I had absolutely no experience in actually collecting money from borrowers. So I decided to cut that number by two-thirds, and bid two cents on the dollar. In other words, for every $100 of loan amount that was still technically outstanding and due the lender from these borrowers, I would pay $2 to buy that loan.

If I then could collect more than $2, I would have recouped my cost and made a profit on the loan. If I collected less, then I would have just done another stupid thing in my life by paying more than I received in return.

Remember that I was completely broke. So for me to say ". . . pay $2 to buy that loan" needs a little explanation. I meant that I would find *someone else* to pay two cents on the dollar.

Where did I go? To the bank I owed a million dollars to, of course!

Yes, I've been accused of insanity more than once. But here was my logic:

- I wanted to pay back that bank. I had no intention of walking away from my debt.
- The bank had a big incentive for me to pay back that million bucks.
- The bank understood the lending business, and would know a thing or two about a portfolio of loans.
- Here we go again with the "ifs": If I could show the bank that I had done a good job in estimating the realistic value in this portfolio of junk debt, then it might just see a small loan to me as its best way to get repaid the bigger loan of $1 million.

I made an appointment with the president of the bank. He knew me all right—I owed him a million bucks!

I filled him in on my recent research in Tulsa, and said: "I think I can collect six cents on the dollar, and I want to put a bid in for two cents on the dollar."

In actual dollar terms, I was saying to him that I thought I could collect $40,000 on this portfolio of loans that were "worth" $670,000, and that I wanted to bid $13,000 for them. If I won the bid—using the bank's money—and if I was right that I could somehow get $40,000 from the defaulted borrowers, then I'd pay the bank back its $13,000. I would then keep $10,000 for my own, and the rest would go toward paying down my $1 million debt.

He looked at my numbers and agreed that maybe—just maybe— somebody could collect $40,000 out of this bucket of loans. With that, he took the next step: He collected all of my handwritten spreadsheets and sent his employee to the Tulsa bank to have him review the loans.

The bank never did tell me what their own employee's analysis revealed, but it must have been consistent with my own estimate, because they went forward with the transaction!

They said, "Okay, we will lend you your bid amount." I was excited. I thought to myself that if I only collected half of the $40,000 then at least my bank would get its $13,000 back and my family could eat a little longer.

I tendered that sealed bid and it was accepted! My bank in Muskogee then cut a check for $13,000 and sent its employee with me to deliver the check to the bank in Tulsa, to finalize the deal. We then literally picked up the box of loan files and I went home with them.

I then began the collection process from my kitchen table. I gave the bank weekly reports of how many people I was able to locate, how many people I in fact contacted, and how I was progressing. It all was relative to the score I had previously assigned. In other words, I measured how responsive each borrower was, compared to my original score.

Once a week I would sit down with my Muskogee bank contact person and show him all of these notes. He would scribble his own notes and make a report to the bank. It took about 60 days for me to work through that entire box of loans and collect the bulk of the money that I thought I'd ever make.

Remember that I thought it would be great if I could get $20,000? And remember how I estimated to myself and to the bank that I might be able to get as much as six cents on the dollar, or $40,000? Well, I collected $63,000!

Everyone was guardedly happy: My banker got his $13,000 back, and another $40,000 went to paying down my million-dollar debt. I kept $10,000 so we could hold off our own bill collectors.

I was feeling pretty good about this. I called the guy who ran that original ad and said, "You got any more of those?"

To my surprise I found out that I was the *only guy* that showed up on the first auction. There were also other packages for sale, and none of the other packages that had been previously offered actually sold.

I'm thinking, "Oh, crap! Either I got like really lucky on a fluke—or maybe I'm about to get really lucky on a regular basis!" I didn't know which way it would go.

I'll continue this story in later chapters, but I want to make sure you see what happened: My billion-dollar business appeared in the newspaper for anyone to run with. It was disguised as a stupid-sounding opportunity.

## The FDIC and the RTC

What I had come across in that small ad in the paper was the world's first public auction for a portfolio of bad debt from a bank. It was to become a flood of debt from two sources: The FDIC and the RTC.

I already introduced you to the FDIC. It's the outfit that regulates banks in America. In the late 1980s, another entity was created by Congress, called the Resolution Trust Corporation.

The RTC came about as a result of the wave of failures in savings and loan institutions in the 1980s. The FDIC had been around for a long time, and was dealing with its own series of bank failures.

There are plenty of books about how these failures occurred, and it doesn't really matter for purposes of our discussion. What matters is how the government entities went about repairing lending institutions, and how it created a win/win opportunity for Yours Truly.

Artists may paint with delicate brushes, and surgeons may repair organs with tiny stitches, but when the government does something, it uses massive, blunt tools.

Look at Figure 2.1. You don't need a PhD in statistics to see that bank and thrift (i.e. savings and loan) failures occurred in two main periods during the last century: There was a huge number of them in the Great Depression, and then a big spike in the 1980s.

Bank health is all about consumer confidence. People are content to leave their money in banks when they think it will be there later for them to take out. When that trust is eroded, all hell breaks loose.

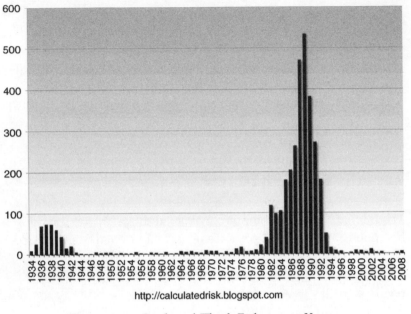

http://calculatedrisk.blogspot.com

FIGURE 2.1    Bank and Thrift Failures per Year

Hence the need for government sometimes to act in very broad, very swift ways. When the giant spike occurred in the 1980s, the government enlisted an army of accountants, analysts, and regulators. They scanned the financial statements of banks and thrifts across the country and identified the institutions that were failing or likely to fail under the weight of too many bad loans. (Let's just call them "banks" from here on.)

They went into those banks and bought bad assets by the dump-truck full. Remember how I went to Tulsa and bought those loans for two cents on the dollar? The regulators did something similar with about $50 billion of loans around the country.

Their interest was not to make a few dollars in order to eat, the way mine had been. The regulators were buying these bad loans in order to inject cash into banks in exchange for the problem assets that had been weighing down those banks.

Why would they do that? Because when a bank is saddled with too many bad loans, it cannot make new loans. Banking regulations became pretty strict after the Great Depression. As we discussed earlier, when loans become delinquent and stay that way, they must be *charged off* and considered worthless.

Banks can only make new loans in certain specific proportions to the amount of good loans on their books. Therefore, every bad loan is not only a pain in the butt for the bank to collect on, but it prevents that bank from earning new fees in the form of new loans.

## Two Important Outcomes of Bank Rescues

After the regulators inject capital into a bank by buying up bad assets, two very important things happen, among many others:

1. *Regulators want to dispose of those assets.* Let's keep in mind where the money comes from when regulators prop up a bank: That's taxpayer money. It may be true that the government is sometimes wasteful and buys $800 coffeepots, as happened in one defense contract. But when we're talking tens of billions of dollars, even the government will sharpen its pencil and try to save a billion or two.

   It does that by recycling the money. After it buys bad assets and saves a bank, it then looks for private buyers of those assets. The government may or may not be able to recoup all of its investment in those assets, but it will try.

   The more successful the government is at selling assets and getting some of its money back, the sooner it can buy still more assets from other troubled banks.

2. *When the government does rescue a bank, other bad loans come out of the woodwork.* Remember how the bank had to "write down" that bass boat of Joe's after it had reached the maximum delinquent period of 120 days? Well, what if a

clever banker approached Joe on day 100 and offered to refinance the loan? Might Joe accept because he would rather not be in default? And wouldn't that prevent the original loan from being written down to zero value on day 120?

Games like this do happen in banking. They're often more subtle than I just described, but even gray-suited bankers can get creative when their companies are at stake.

When those bankers are bailed out by the government, they often want to "clean house" of other bad loans at the same time. Because their financial statements have been strengthened, they are in a position to play hardball with Joe and let that loan reach day 120 after all.

Therefore the very act of the government buying a large portfolio of assets has a way of dumping an even larger overall amount of bad loans on the market.

## When I Realized I'd Seen This Movie Before

In addition to becoming a very major purchaser of many billions of dollars in bad debt in the 1990s, my company had also worked closely with the RTC as a repackager of its loans to buyers across the country. I intimately knew the entire process the RTC used to dispose of assets.

I've given you all this background because now you might begin to see what I saw about just the first $700 billion government bailout plan in late 2008. In rough outlines, here were the facts:

- Banks are saddled with bad debts from consumers and elsewhere.
- They were required to write off those bad loans.
- The act of writing off the loans meant those banks could not lend as much money as they otherwise could.
- Lending between banks was drying up, to the point where they not only wouldn't lend to consumers, but would not even lend to each other.

- The $700 billion bailout would buy interests in banks across the country.
- Those stabilized banks could then discharge the worst of their assets by discounting them heavily and selling them to investors. This would happen as quickly as possible, because Congress wanted reassurance that taxpayers would get some of that $700 billion back.

The similarities were astonishing. And as we know, under the new Obama Administration, we've seen another stimulus bill of roughly $800 billion signed into law, with talk of the full bailout reaching $2.5 trillion.

Yet at the same time, there are important differences between what I experienced in the 1990s and what we're seeing today. The differences relate to the size of the opportunity, and the speed with which it is going to wash over America.

## A Perfect Storm of Financial Factors

I know the term *perfect storm* has been used a lot, but sometimes it really does work as a description.

Individual storms happen frequently. It's quite rare for two large storms to hit at the same time. For three storms to hit simultaneously and strengthen each other, now that's worth making a movie about.

In the case of the situation we have as you are reading this book, several financial storms are gathering and gaining strength.

### Storm #1: Lack of Infrastructure

Look back at Figure 2.1. See how every year there has been some tiny number of bank failures, and then we have the proverbial "pig in a python" in the Great Depression and in the 1980s?

Year in and year out, a few banks go under for whatever reason. The government maintains a very small infrastructure to deal with these banks. It's the same with collection agencies: In any given year, only so many agencies exist because there's enough activity to keep them in business, but not enough to keep twice as many firms in business.

Figure 2.1 shows the two spikes in the early and late parts of the last century, but it does not show the current crisis. If it did, the bank failure spike would blow a hole in the top of the chart, both in terms of number of banks and dollar volume.

I can assure you that the infrastructure needed to handle the current bank restructuring is not in place.

What does that do to the market? It drops prices. It all has to do with value versus price.

The value of the bad loans is what it is. Maybe they're only worth a dime or 15 cents or 20 cents on the dollar. That doesn't change quickly. The thing that changes is what people will pay for that package of loans, based on how rare or plentiful they are.

In the space of a few months in 2008, oil was $147 a barrel and then dropped below $40. Its consistency, viscosity, lubricating power, volume, stickiness, and smelliness all stayed the same. It's a barrel of oil. Its properties didn't change, but the price radically changed.

In the world of buying bad debt, price swings can be even greater than what we've seen with oil recently.

If the FDIC has loans that are worth 20 cents on the dollar in a very efficient marketplace, people will come in and pay close to 20 cents on the dollar, minus their collection costs. In our current environment, with enormous swings in the capacity of firms to absorb this bad debt coming onto the market, it's possible to pay ridiculously low prices as compared to the value.

It won't always be this way, mind you. At some point—my guess is a few years after this book comes out—there will be more companies to handle the bad debt than there is debt to be handled. That's just the nature of the beast.

Right now, there's no competition at all.

## Storm #2: Size of the Problem

I know what you're thinking! "But Bill, that might be true when you wrote this book; what about now, when I'm reading it? Could there now be enough firms to handle the debt?"

The answer is no. Remember the Frito-Lay commercial that used to run? It said: "Go ahead . . . we're making more!" If you think this problem is over some months or even a couple of years after this book was published, you're living in a fantasy world.

Here's how I know: We've only had the first wave of acknowledgment of the trouble we're in. But there's a second wave—the one they haven't yet shown us. It's either because they're not coming clean with the public, or they don't know the magnitude of the problem themselves. Same difference.

Don't believe me? Let's go back to recent history and look at the subprime meltdown. In early 2008 the banking industry voluntarily set aside $100 billion to deal with the "subprime problem." About 45 days later they said, "Oh, we might want to make that $200 billion," and they did.

The institutions created reserves to deal with that among themselves, without government involvement. Then, lo and behold, along comes the $700 billion to deal with the same subprime meltdown, followed by another $800 billion, with talk of trillions before we're done.

This problem is so gigantic that when the automobile industry got a $25 billion bailout in October of 2008, nobody saw it. A mere $25 billion barely made the newspaper.

Let me put it another way: Whatever they're showing us presently, there is at least that much behind the curtain. They probably recognize it, but do not yet have the courage to admit that difficult message. If they did, it could create panic on the streets. Wall Street has been paranoid enough, just with the current bailout amounts.

Remember that other phenomenon I mentioned earlier: As banks get a portion of the hundreds of billions, it enables them to "fess up" to more bad loans. An infusion of $1 billion into a bank allows them to write off another $1 billion worth of otherwise questionable loans that they were in denial about. They couldn't admit they were as bad as they were, because if they did, their capital ratio would go upside down. And if your capital ratio goes upside down, you are a failed bank.

There's another reason the banks want to clear this nasty stuff off their books: It allows them to become more efficient and to allocate their resources more appropriately. They become better-run institutions in an industry that is going to be riddled with casualties.

Even bankers realize that the bank that can run most efficiently ends up being the last bank standing. In the late 1980s, there were 14,000 banks. There are now about 8,000 banks. As you may have heard, the government is choosing which banks it wants to rescue, and which others it will let wither and die, to get gobbled up by stronger banks. It's happening as we speak.

## Storm #3: Urgency to Solve the Problem

Barack Obama was voted into office for lots of reasons, but everyone can agree that the economy was one of the biggest ones. At the time of the election, absolutely nothing dominated the news the way the economy did. We witnessed wild swings in the stock market, the failure of major institutions, and talk that ranged from "recession" to "depression" and "catastrophe."

The Democrats now control both houses of Congress and the executive branch. They have two years until the mid-term elections. They only need to look back to Bill Clinton, the last Democrat president, to see what happens if the country is dissatisfied after you've been in office for two years—the country handed firm control of Congress to the Republicans.

Democrats are highly unlikely to put themselves in a position where that can happen again. One of the most effective ways to prevent that is to be able to say, two years from now, "We cleaned up that mess the Republicans left us."

I'm not taking sides here, though I have my own opinions. I'm simply stating with absolute certainty that the command coming down to the Treasury Department from the President and Congress will be: "Fix this fast."

There will be much greater urgency to spend that bailout/stimulus money quickly and institute a "colon cleanse" of those 8,000 banks just as quickly as humanly possible—and maybe even *quicker than possible.*

In that case, urgency will cascade throughout the system from top to bottom. The message will be: "Don't sweat the price we get for bad assets—just move that inventory out!"

Just what do you suppose that will do to the price?

Given the magnitude of the problem, I expect it will take the full two years to wash these bad loans out of thousands of banks. It may even take longer. Sooner or later, all "good" things come to an end.

I suggest you act now, while the magnitude of the problem is at its greatest, the facilities to handle the problem are at their lowest, and there's an extreme willingness to do what it takes to get it solved.

## Storm #4: The Seller Is Not the Owner

If you own your house free and clear with no mortgage, then you're likely to care about what it sells for. The same is true if you're a craftsman who builds chairs or you bake pies for a living.

But what if your job is simply to move inventory?

I am not referring to theory. This is how bad asset sales work. How do I know? I sold literally billions of dollars of assets for the RTC. Here's the deal.

Acme Financial Services applies to be a sales agent for the regulators. The feds do their paper pushing and let's say they decide to make Acme one of its agents. Acme is given a big portfolio of loans. It is then given three mandates:

1. Sell those loans.

2. Sell those loans.

3. *Try* to sell them somewhere within an established price range.

That's it. Acme does *not* get paid on commission, based on how much it sells the assets for.

If Acme reports back, "We only got the minimum for those portfolios of assets, but we sold 'em," they're told, "Well done. Here's another bunch to sell."

If Acme says, "Great news! We got *double* what we thought we could get for those assets, but only sold 80 percent of them! That's way more money we recovered for the taxpayers," they'll likely be told, "You're fired."

Oh, and did I mention who sets the price range? Acme does. Before the sales take place, Acme will analyze the loans and come up with that range. It then gets approval by the regulators.

Given that Acme knows full well the three mandates it has, what kind of price range do you suppose Acme will establish? Will it be a highly aggressive one that will yield the most return for taxpayers, or an OK-to-low one that ensures the inventory gets moved?

I can see you're catching on.

## Storm #5: We Are Not Talking Just Home Loans

If you have been listening to the news and are now reading this book, I can see another question rattling around in your brain:

> "But Bill, the press is only talking about the subprime mortgage mess and home foreclosures. Yet you made your billion bucks off unsecured loans like credit card debt. Am I right that the current opportunity is *not* in those nice, cheap, toxic loans you got so good at collecting on?"

No, you would not be right. The current opportunity is about billions of dollars of every type of loan imaginable.

Let's revisit our friend Joe, who formerly was the proud owner of his BassBuster bass boat. Joe has still not found a job, and he's way past thinking about bass fishing. Things are getting serious. He owns a house, a pickup truck, and a few bass trophies.

When he can't get employment but the bills keep coming, he sells those trophies on eBay. What goes next?

It would have to be the truck. When faced with the bad choice of a truck and no home, or a home and no truck, Joe will stay in his home. He can bum a ride off someone. Plus he's not working, so commuting is not an issue.

The truck goes, and that keeps Joe afloat for a little longer. When things don't improve, Joe mails the keys back to the bank that holds his home mortgage and walks out the door.

Let's examine what we know about Joe in the context of what we're hearing about the economy. In the space of a few months in late 2008 and early 2009, we had about $1.5 trillion in bailout/ stimulus money printed up, primarily due to the subprime mortgage mess. Houses were foreclosed on in record numbers. Wall Street's suspender-clad geniuses bet wrong and lost it all, and now the government is picking up the pieces.

For us to get into hundreds of billions of dollars worth of bad home loans—how many bass boats and pickup trucks do you suppose first had to get towed away?

What we are seeing with the government bailout is merely the hunk of the iceberg that is sticking out of the water. There is a much bigger hunk underwater, in the form of all the property that people have let slide into foreclosure before they give up their houses.

As just one example, *The Nilson Report* is a research company in the credit card industry. It recently published a prediction that the volume of credit card charge-offs is likely to go up by 50 percent in the next two years and equal $340 billion.

## In the Next Chapter

Forget a perfect storm with a mere three separate powerful forces coming together at one time. We have five.

Forget James Marshall finding a few nuggets of gold at Sutter's Mill. If you add up the entire estimated amount of gold mined during the California Gold Rush and convert it to the *current* price of gold, in today's dollars it amounts to less than $9 billion.

This bad-debt opportunity is the *true* gold rush, and it's the world's best-kept secret, right out in the open.

Let's now examine how you might be one of the first prospectors on the scene.

# Understand That You Can Take Advantage of It, Regardless of Your Circumstances

In the previous chapter, I established the enormity of the opportunity in front of you. In a sense, it's even bigger than Bill Gates standing in Harvard Square with that famous copy of *Popular Science* in his hand, staring at a crude personal computer on the cover. Gates had to invent new software and wait years to develop his opportunity to the fullest.

In your case, there's nothing to invent, and the opportunity is right here, right now.

My Sixth Sense for Questions is kicking in again, and I can hear you saying:

> Well, Bill, I'm intrigued. But this time I have a very basic, fundamental question for you: If it's such a good opportunity, why am I not hearing it plastered all over the media?

That's an excellent question. Fortunately for you, I have an excellent answer:

This opportunity is completely camouflaged by layer upon layer of objection, misconception, and myth. Any single one of these negatives is enough to turn away many people and businesses. Put them all together and you're looking at a gauntlet that will keep away all but a handful of extremely savvy people, who are soon to be extremely rich.

Having laid out for you the opportunity, it's now important to walk into the gauntlet and address each obstacle in your way. Let's get started.

> Are you suggesting that I become a screaming, pestering, threatening kneecap-breaker of a bill collector?

No.

In my 12 years of working this business, I certainly never was that. In fact, in my company, it was grounds for instant firing to be anything but courteous to people.

I have to explain something about myself. There are many aspects about my upbringing that I wish I could change: The gang association, the fights and alcoholism, the disappointment that I brought to many people who knew me—I could go on.

I readily acknowledge that there are others who are smarter, taller, more handsome, and stronger than I am. As the 25th-richest person in America, I knew there were 24 people who were even richer than I was. But there's one area where I am an absolute authority; I know what it's like to be desperately poor:

- I've literally been ankle-deep in hot blood in the slaughterhouse room where I would slit the throats of pigs for a few bucks an hour, with no benefits.
- I've eaten out of Dumpsters for weeks at a time. I lived an entire summer in a hayloft until one day the farmer found my clothes and burned them.
- On the occasions when I was in business and lost it all—that's more than once—I would be hounded relentlessly by bill collectors. I literally tore the phone out of the wall once, after being awakened and threatened by a collector.

I know for a fact that I made a billion dollars because in the nasty industry of bill collection, I created an island of respectful, polite problem solvers instead of bill collectors.

That is not personal delusion on my part. I didn't create such an environment because I think I'm holier than everyone else. I did it because it was very smart business.

My livelihood consisted of getting portfolios of loans. Banks sold them to me for two reasons:

1. I paid for the loans;
2. I would not bring bad publicity to their companies.

If they made a few bucks selling their toxic waste loans to me, and then read in the press about their borrowers being hounded and threatened, they would be the ones with the black eye.

Don't get me wrong: It wasn't that they cared so much about their borrowers. They didn't. It's that they did not want bad press associated with their name. As far as everyone was concerned, it was the bank collecting on the loans, and not some outfit they sold the loans to.

I wanted more business from these banks so I made sure I had the best reputation, along with a fair price for the loans.

You want proof of my reputation?

- An article in *USA Today* labeled us the "kinder, gentler approach to bill collecting."
- We received the Better Business Bureau "Torch Award for Ethics in the Marketplace." Think about that: Bill collectors usually rank somewhere below used car dealers and politicians for ethics. We got a national award for our business ethics.
- *The Nilson Report* (industry newsletter) said we were the largest, best-trained, and most efficient collection operation in the world.
- *Business Week* named us as one of the top 100 family-friendly companies.
- *Working Mother Magazine* gave us a similar award for being a great environment for mothers.

In case you think it's easy for only a big company to do that—but not if you are starting out—that's not the case. Because of my history on the receiving end of bad bill collectors, I made sure that my very first call from that kitchen table to a borrower was polite and respectful.


## A Secret about Dealing with Borrowers

Let's revisit Joe the bass fisherman. Joe's boat is gone, the truck is being hauled away as we speak, and his seven credit cards are long since maxed out. He took cash advances on the new ones to pay the minimum on the old ones—until there were no more cash advances.

Now Joe wakes up every morning to three new calls on his answering machine, plus calls on his cell phone and every other known number. That doesn't count all the letters.

Joe is being hounded from every direction. He owes $1,950 a month in total just for minimum payments, never mind paying off the balances. He can only scrape together $310 a month to pay such bills by working at his brother-in-law's scrap yard.

Bill Bartmann's collection company reaches Joe on the phone, and Joe instinctively closes his eyes as he awaits the barrage of browbeating and threats.

Joe opens his eyes. He's not being beat up. Hey, wait—is this a collection company after all? Sure doesn't sound like one. They're actually listening to Joe's story about how he was downsized from that lousy company he gave 15 years of good service to.

They're respectful and they listen. They also offer to think creatively about how Joe might be able to piece some things together in his life.

The next month, Joe has a decision to make: Toward which bill do I apply my lousy 310 bucks—the threatening browbeaters, or that Bill Bartfield guy who actually was pleasant to talk with?

I can tell you for a documented fact—from my company collecting many billions of dollars in overdue loans—that Joe will *pay the nice people first*, and the rest can stand in line and wait their turn.

This is not theory. This is how I made a billion dollars.

Okay, that sounds a lot better than what I had been thinking. But still, do I have any alternative other than to pick up the phone myself and make these calls?

Yes, you do. I'll talk about this in much greater depth in a later chapter, but you can hire a collection company to make the calls for you.

I was the pioneer in compassionate collecting, but nowadays there are a few companies that have figured out what I did many years ago. I'll show you how to find them.

> Bill, if these companies are actually good at collecting, why would they want to work for me, collecting on my portfolio of loans? Why wouldn't they just buy and work their own loans?

I can tell you from 12 years of being in the collection business that the vast majority of companies did one or the other, but not both: They either worked their own portfolios or they collected for other companies. It's just the way it is.

Companies tend to specialize and get good at their own little niche. Did Bill Gates have the brains and money to get involved in selling computers as well as his software? Of course. But he decided to specialize in just the software. There was enough money to be made right where he was.

> The biggest roadblock I have to even considering this business is that I'm broke myself! How can I possibly "invest" in a portfolio of loans if I'm trying to find the money to invest in food to eat?

Remember the shape I was in when I started this business: I was a million bucks in the hole. I didn't have the money to take the toll road, so I took the back roads in my friend's car from Muskogee to Tulsa.

In a later chapter I explain how you can get 100 percent financing for your portfolio of loans—from a standing start, with no experience in this business, and no connections. I know how, because I did it.

I wouldn't know where to begin.

That's the purpose of this book. First you must understand the opportunity, and then understand that you can take advantage of it. At that point we'll roll up our sleeves and discuss every step you take, in the correct order, to get your first portfolio of loans.

What if I simply have no time to work these loans?

I have two answers for you: First, you can farm out the working of the loans to a collection agency, as I mentioned above.

Second, you can make time. Remember that I started this business when I was desperately working to try to put food on the table. After my pipe company collapsed when the price of oil collapsed, I went into business at a trucking firm.

It sounds like I was back on my feet, but I really wasn't. The trucking firm's customers were people in the oil business, and they were all dying. So on paper I would share in profits from this company. In reality, we had no paying customers and I banged the phones all day long, usually making no money at it.

To put things in perspective, I spent one year working more than full time, and made less than $10,000 for my efforts.

It's in that context that I found time at night and on weekends to make calls on my little box of loans. I could have taken longer to do it—I owned those loans. It's just that I had this gnawing feeling in my gut that I needed to make the calls sooner rather than later. That "gnawing feeling" was a lack of food.

I've been in one business or another for the last four decades. I don't care who you are—there are always a few minutes available to do something if you consider it important.

If you have more money than you have time, then hire people to make the calls for you. If you have more time than money, you do it yourself.

If you have neither time nor money, you have a decision to make: Where am I spending my time, and is it making more money for me than those calls would? Until you see a flow of dough coming in from those calls, you simply have to test it out and see for yourself.

When I started, I had 100 reasons why my idea would never work. I went ahead because I realized that I had no better options, and I'd soon know if this business was for real, or not.

I suggest you do the same.

## But Bill, I don't have enough education and experience.

Wait a minute: Do you think you start in this business after going to Compassionate Bill Collector University? You start by starting.

There are not many moving parts to the business, after all: You buy a portfolio of loans, using someone else's money. You contact the borrowers and ask certain specific questions, and take good notes.

You follow through until you either get some or all of the money, or you satisfy yourself that you will not get any more. You then "lather, rinse, and repeat," as they say.

Let me put it to you a different way:

At certain times when I was building my business, I literally was hiring 70 people *per week*. I had 3,900 employees and couldn't grow fast enough. Given that I was hiring people to work from Tulsa and not Manhattan, it's not like I could be too picky about whom I hired. Therefore I tried to be flexible in my criteria. Even so, I had one rock-solid rule for hiring:

If you had any experience as a bill collector, no thanks. We would not even consider you for the job.

Why? Because there's a very good chance you would already be mentally polluted with the hardball tactics other firms use to stomp on borrowers. In my experience, based on hiring thousands of people, the only good collector was the beginner, whom I could train to do the job the right way.

So if you have no experience—welcome. If you do have experience in bill collecting as you read this, um, perhaps you should close this book now, sell it on eBay, and go do something else.

> You're suggesting that I go into business, but I don't have an office or any employees, and don't even look the part!

Don't make me reach through this page and knock you upside the head! Have you been paying attention?

You *do not* need an office or employees when you're starting out in this business. Those are just other terms for "overhead." I'm a big believer in keeping your overhead (monthly expenses) as low as possible until you start seeing nice monthly revenue.

There will be plenty of time to grow later. In fact, I devote an entire chapter to the topic of making your business as large as you wish. For now, just forget about all the trappings of being in business.

Got a phone, pencil, and a pad of paper? Congratulations: You're in business.

> Okay, Bill, I'm beginning to see that just maybe I could do this business, or at least try it out. But I have yet another nagging question: Even you must admit that I would start out as "small potatoes." Why should I expect to see any decent loans at all? Wouldn't they have long since been picked over by others, leaving me with the dregs?

That's a good question. The answer has to do with the concepts of "price" and "value."

Let's consider that very first portfolio of loans I found in the paper in Muskogee. The *face value* of the loans in that portfolio was around $670,000. In other words, at the time of borrowing, those borrowers had promised to pay back their entire loans to the tune of $670,000.

That was before all the hardships.

At the time when those loans were late but not by much, the value of that portfolio would have dropped. Then doubt crept in about whether the loans would be repaid, and stories were beginning to emerge about layoffs, sickness, and so on.

As time went on, the collection efforts resulted in some loans being repaid, and those were taken out of the portfolio. They were "settled." The collectors continued to try to collect, and the non-payers continued not to pay.

After multiple tries by the bank, and then attempts by at least three different collection agencies, the bank put that ad in the newspaper for anyone to bid on the portfolio.

As you will recall, I bid $13,000, or 2 percent of the face value of those loans. The bank accepted my bid. Looking at it another way, this portfolio was certainly not worth $670,000, but it was not worthless, either. It was close to worthless, though. The bank had satisfied itself that every attempt had been made at collecting from these particularly difficult remaining borrowers—with no success. So the bank figured 2 percent was better than 0 percent.

Even ignorant beginner Bill Bartmann was aware that these loans had been picked over and worked, big time. I could see the dozens of documented attempts in each file.

But by paying (or rather, getting the bank to pay) $13,000 for this portfolio, I had just dropped the success bar way way down. I didn't need to collect 670 grand in order to get my money back; I just had to collect 13 grand!

When the *price* dropped low enough, the *value* to me of that portfolio increased. At a price of almost zero, it was now worth my while to try to collect on those hardship stories. As you know, I collected $63,000. That represented a phenomenal return on my small investment.

To be technical about it, I received an infinite percent return, because I put up no money—the bank did. I made my 10 grand and the bank got the rest, in exchange for investing that $13,000.

So yes, you will see ugly loans. But understand that the prettier the loans, the more you will pay for them. Do you want pretty loans that badly? Or do you want the ugly ones that cost so little?

Another billionaire made his name in a similar fashion. Ross Perot worked for IBM in sales. He got very good at selling, and one day had an idea. He approached his sales manager and asked that he be given all the crappy accounts. In other words, Ross wanted all the accounts that every other salesman (they were all men at the time) had tried to sell, but to no avail.

The manager shrugged and let Ross try to sell them. Which he did. He was a natural, plus he worked very hard. As you probably know, salespeople are usually assigned quotas for a given period. In the case of IBM, salesmen had an annual number they had to meet in order to be considered successful.

By taking on these toughest of accounts, and getting as good as he got, Ross Perot would fulfill his annual sales quota—by January 3!

(To finish that story, when he approached IBM with the concept for a new business and they said, "No, thanks," he founded his own firm and proceeded to make his billions.)

The bottom line of all this: "Tough" is your friend, if you can buy it cheaply enough.

Bill, I understand the concept of "small," but I'm only one guy. Is it actually possible for a portfolio of loans to be packaged and made available to a one-person shop?

Yes. Remember—I was one person. And that was no fluke. In fact, the FDIC and RTC both had a mandate to make this opportunity available for average citizens to participate. Both agencies were required to package loans not so large as to exclude the small guy.

From my knowledge of the new legislation relating to the current bailout, the government is following the same principle.

Also please keep in mind that size becomes less of an issue when you're not putting up any dough. Then you can truly afford to take a larger portfolio, as long as it's not so large that you can't even get to all the borrowers in that portfolio.

> I understand that you had a tough start in life, Bill, but at least you're a white man. You don't have the extra burdens in the business world that are created by being a woman or being a minority in our society.

I don't disagree with that statement. As tough as I had it growing up, I realize other people have their own tough stories to tell. I have two responses:

1. Don't let your background stand in the way of your success. Are you going to be content with failing, and having lots of excuses to point to as to why you failed? Or will you succeed in spite of whatever challenges you have?

2. Sometimes the government actually makes some smart moves. In the case of bad loan portfolios, they made a good one: There is special, favorable treatment available to women, minorities, and veterans.

I have it right here in a document straight off the United States Treasury web site: It's called the "Process for Selecting Asset Managers Pursuant to the Emergency Economic Stabilization Act of 2008." And I quote:

## Small and Minority- and Women-Owned Businesses

The Treasury will issue separate notices, consistent with these procedures, specifically to identify smaller and minority- and women-owned Financial Institutions that do not meet the minimum qualifications for current assets under management in the initial notices. Such Financial Institutions will be designated as sub-managers within the portfolio.

In other words, these groups will not directly work with the government, but they'll be "sub-managers" under the bigger outfits which will have those direct pipelines to the government.

You know how the government just loves acronyms that spell stuff? Well, they're having a field day with this new legislation. Here's a piece of a document from the "Department of the Treasury's Emergency Economic Stabilization Act Procurements Small Business Participation":

There are **no requirements under this authority to set-aside procurements** for small (including small business concerns owned and controlled by veterans (VOSBs), small business concerns owned and controlled by service-disabled veterans (SDVOSBs), certified HUB-Zone small business concerns (HUBZones), certified small business concerns owned and controlled by socially and economically disadvantaged individuals (SDBs), and small business concerns owned and controlled by women (WOSBs), woman- and minority-owned businesses; however, the Department of the Treasury has included these groups as part of the selection process. **If small businesses determine that they do not meet the minimum requirements stated in the notices, they may participate as subcontractors.** [*I added the emphasis.*]

Your tax dollars at work! Let me translate the above: If you are a veteran, disabled vet, small business owner, woman business owner, or a socially and economically disadvantaged person, they're saying, "Don't worry if you do not meet our regular requirements; we'll try to fit you in as a subcontractor."

Remember the politics attached to the bailout/stimulus plan: Congress wants to make sure it gets lots of great publicity about how the money didn't just go to Wall Street, but went to Main Street, too. That was the whole focus of discussion at the late stages of the presidential campaign, and no one disagreed.

Because I packaged over $6 billion in loans for the government, let me tell you from the inside how this process works.

Let's say I'm selling a portfolio of loans for the government, and I have three bidders. They're sealed bids, so no one knows what the other person has bid. The minimum bid level for this portfolio has already been set at $21,000. Here's what happens:

> Ralph, white guy, bids $22,500;
> Marvin, white guy, bids $24,750;
> Maria, Hispanic woman, bids $20,000.

I would most likely award this portfolio to Maria. She didn't meet the minimum bid, but I—the packaging agent for the government—have other fish to fry. I need to show that my packages were bought by a variety of special groups over the course of the last month. This month has been lean, in the sense that mostly big companies and white guys have been my buyers.

Besides, Maria's bid wasn't $4,000. If she had bid that, she would not win. But at $20,000, Maria's bid was only a little below my minimum of $21,000. It's therefore Maria's lucky day.

That is how the system worked before, and it worked quite well. I have no reason to believe the government will do anything different this time around.

Interesting note: In my capacity as a packager for the government at times, I saw many bidders who were clueless about these special groups. They most likely would have qualified, had they known about them and filled out a few forms. They didn't have a book like the one you're holding that would show them the ropes.

> I've been watching the government bailout pretty closely, and I know they're still working out the details of how all this will work. We all know how slowly the government does things. Must I keep waiting for all those programs to get up and running before I start to see packages of loans?

You do not have to wait. You can get a portfolio of loans *today*.

First, as I described in the previous chapter, the current bailout is only the tip of the iceberg when it comes to bad loans available in the marketplace.

Second, several hundred billion dollars has already been dispensed by Congress to the Treasury Department to buy interests in banks around the country. Much of that money went to prop up the banks, which are now intent on shoving their bad loans out the door quickly.

Third, even if there had not been a government bailout, there has already been a mountain of bad debt hitting the market. As I said earlier, it's projected that credit card companies alone will charge off $340 billion in card balances over the next two years, up 50 percent from the previous period. Not to mention Joe's bass boat and a few hundred million other cars and toys.

In a later chapter, I describe precisely how to find and acquire these different types of portfolios.

> Bill, this all sounds pretty good, but I have to challenge you once again: *Nothing* is great for everyone. Everything has pros and cons. For whom is this *not* a good opportunity?

Very fair question. I agree that nothing is right for everyone, and I'm always suspicious of promoters who make an opportunity sound that way.

The good news is there are many things that do *not* matter in the least:

- Age or gender doesn't matter.
- No one cares about the color of your skin.
- Lack of income is no big deal.
- Lack of experience is actually better than thinking you know something about this business.
- Education or lack of it is irrelevant.
- Where you live doesn't matter.
- Whatever you may be running away from is your business; no one cares.
- Physical disabilities are irrelevant as long as you can speak and take basic notes.

However, there are four essential personality traits that make it much easier to succeed in this business, based on my experience with literally thousands of employees. Notice that I said "personality traits." They are things you ultimately do have control over. Let's look at the short list:

- A *few hours per week of your time*. You may think this is not a personality trait, but it is. People find time to do the things they care about, and make excuses about being "way too busy" for things they don't care about.

    I paid cash for a $25 million Gulfstream IV jet, because I was that busy and valued my time that much. Yet I admit that if I had wanted to take up a hobby like painting or woodworking, I could have carved out a few hours per week.

    On the other end of the spectrum, when I was going to community college during the day and working at the slaughterhouse at night, even then I could find an hour here and a half hour there for things I wanted to do.

Sorry if this comes across as harsh, but if you're bellyaching about lack of time, you are making that argument to the wrong guy at the moment. It says to me that you don't want the reward badly enough.

• *The ability to follow a process.* Artists and free thinkers are great. They make our world a much nicer place in which to live. Too bad their talents are wasted on portfolios of bad loans.

This is not a complicated business. Furthermore, I reduced the business down to a science. As I told you before, the collection industry's main trade journal called my operation the most efficient in the world.

If you're the sort of person who gets itchy with doing the same thing in the same way over and over—even if it's yielding good results—go to art school instead.

• *The ability to step outside of your comfort zone just a little bit.* I recognize that I'm absolutely fearless about trying new things and stepping out of my comfort zone. I also recognize that I'm unusual in that regard. Maybe it's all the crazy things that have happened to me.

Fortunately, you don't have to be that fearless. You just have to accept a small level of discomfort.

You don't need to go door-to-door and have the doors slammed in your face. You don't need to run for public office and risk losing after months of hard work. You simply need to be able to pick up the phone, follow a process, and not be surprised if you don't hit a home run each time.

The first stage is the hardest, because you know the least, you aren't sure of yourself, you've put in time and effort, and don't have any financial rewards to show for it all.

That changes quickly, though. When I started to call people on that first portfolio of bad loans, within days I saw results. Please understand that these people resisted dozens of calls before mine, from multiple "professionals." These borrowers had become professional non-payers.

Yet soon I saw that if I picked up the phone in the comfort of my kitchen, and flapped my lips in a certain way, money would appear in my mailbox. That gave me plenty of incentive to flap my lips some more, to make more money appear.

The same will happen to you, if you put yourself out there and try.

- *The willingness to stick with it when challenges arise.* This may be the biggest one of all. There are two kinds of people: The ones who look for excuses, and the ones who look for footholds.

   As I said, we all are pretty creative at finding reasons why something won't work. That's useful when you want to wallow in pity and get nowhere in life. It's easier to say to yourself, "It's not my fault, because [fill in the blank]; besides, just as I was about to do it, [fill in the blank]."

   It takes a different—and superior—type of skill to say: "Well, that didn't work. But I learned that if I [fill in the blank], then it seems to work better."

   Or you say: "I have to work until after 9:00 PM at my current lousy job, so I can't reach these people at night . . . but maybe if I can swap shifts with Vinnie twice a week, I can then make some calls."

   You encounter an obstacle, then you take out your trusty pocket knife and carve a little hole where you can jam your foot in there and give yourself a leg up to the next level.

Another fellow billionaire, Walter Annenberg, founded a media empire including publications like *TV Guide*. Here's what he said about success:

"I want to remind you that success in life is based on hard slogging. There will be periods when discouragement is great and upsetting, and the antidote for this is calmness and fortitude and a modest yet firm belief in your competence.

"Be sure that your priorities are in order so that you can proceed in a logical manner, and be ever mindful that nothing will take the place of persistence."

I couldn't agree more.

### How much rejection are you asking me to take?

Very little. If you actually prepare, I expect you not to have any.

I'm being absolutely dead serious. Relating to getting the portfolio in the first place, if you follow my specific steps on how to approach suppliers, how to present yourself, and the exact documents you put in front of them, I really don't expect you to be rejected.

Now, will you start at the wrong place sometimes and be rejected because you're asking the wrong guy for something he can't give you? Of course. Even my company got "no" on occasion. That happens in life. Sometimes it's your fault and sometimes it's their fault.

Regarding the process of dealing with borrowers, you'll soon discover that this is a real numbers game. You may get a "no," but you'll very quickly understand exactly what action you then take. Sometimes that action will relate to how you'll deal with that borrower. Other times it will be to know when to move on to the next person.

Your clarity on the next action means that you'll simply not bother with worrying about how the last conversation went. You'll already be focused on the next one.

### But, Bill, I don't deserve to be rich.

I think it's not right for you to feel that way, but I can understand how it happens:

- You may have had a teacher or family member tell you that you'll never amount to anything.

- Perhaps you get the feeling that any time you do well, someone close to you thinks: "Who do you think you are? You think you're better than I am?" "Why should you succeed and leave me behind?" and so on.

You are going to have to sort this out for yourself. Again, how badly do you want to succeed? And if you have friends or relatives who are holding you back and dragging you down, what might you do about that?

I know you can't change friends and relatives quite as quickly as you change underwear, but you can take steps in that direction. If you have such people around you:

- *Don't tell them your plans.* Keep your mouth shut. Or if you know you'll be interrogated, make up some cover story in advance. Say you're investing in mutual funds or you're in a multi-level marketing scheme selling tropical fruit juices. I know!—tell them that you're selling insurance on the side, and ask if they would be interested in talking about insurance policies. That's sure to make them change the topic.

- *Don't ask them for advice.* Then at least they can't say, "Hey, you asked my opinion."

- *Keep quiet about your successes.* This is a good practice, no matter whom you're dealing with. It's no accident that the cover of *Inc.* magazine showed me with one hand over my face, and the headline: "The Billionaire No One Knows." I was making such a bloody fortune at my business that I was quite content to have the very fewest people know about my business. Eventually of course, it was hard to keep quiet when my employees filled a

60-story building. But I can assure you that as long as I could, when people asked me about my line of work, I would just mumble something vague and quickly change the subject.

- *When you become successful, consider giving back.* It's no accident that Mother Teresa said, "Bill Bartmann has made a profound difference in the lives of so many." Bill Cosby said, "Bill is living proof that business success and family values are not incompatible. He has demonstrated the more you give, the more you get."

I found that whatever I put into the community, I got back in spades. It went a long way toward making me feel okay about being rich, believe me.

## Billionaire Principle: You Can't Fail at Trying

You don't have to succeed at first; you simply have to try.

If you're doing emergency brain surgery, then I hope you get it right the first time. But even brain surgeons start off by working on dead people, then work their way up to simple operations on live people, and so on.

Don't fall into the trap of focusing on perfection, or focusing even on doing something well. At first, simply focus on doing. Get out there and try. Screw up, laugh it off, and try it again.

In baseball, the rule is "three strikes and you're out." That's fine for baseball, but we're in a peculiar sort of *money baseball.*

In our version, you get to swing as many times as you wish. It's true that you'll never get anywhere at money baseball if you sit on your butt in the bleachers, eating hot dogs. But if you step into the batter's box and take a swing, no one can call you "out."

Just keep swinging. Eventually you will connect with that ball. Eventually your little base hits will become towering home runs.

Thank your lucky stars that all these misconceptions and myths continue to shroud this amazing opportunity we've been discussing.

If they didn't, we'd have millions more competitors, and profits would go to hell.

## In the Next Chapter

By now you know the enormous magnitude of the opportunity before us. I've also just taken a bulldozer to all those barriers that were standing between where you are and making big money in this business.

Even so, I don't expect you to quit your job tomorrow and grab yourself a box of loans. The cynicism of "It'll never work" is the attitude of losers and failures. The guarded optimism of "I'll give it a try" is the attitude of winners.

Assuming you're in the latter camp, let's proceed to the next chapter and dive into how you get your first portfolio.

# How to Find Good Deals, Part One

I t's time for us to locate your first portfolio of loans. I say "locate" because we'll talk in detail later about how to negotiate and finance your portfolio. For now, it's important to understand some of the dynamics behind the lending business as they relate to the activities you'll soon engage in.

## Various Types of Loans

When you are buying portfolios of loans, they will have a certain amount of similarity within a given portfolio. You won't have a couple of residential mortgages, a few cars, and an office building. That would be mixing the species, so to speak. Let's look at the main distinctions between loan species:

## Small Business Loans

Open your phone book. You'll see every type of business listed in there. They all need loans, whether they're your local doctor, dentist, plumber, or baker. They use that money to finance new equipment, as operating capital between payments for larger work they do, and for many other purposes. These are "main street loans."

When banks make such loans, they tend to hold onto that paper. ("Paper" is shorthand for "loan." You probably heard it referred to during Congressional debate on the bailout. The focus was on "commercial paper," and how those loans had dried up for businesses. Commercial paper is a different breed of loan from what you will be investing in, but you now know the lingo.)

As I was saying, the bank does not sell that business loan to anyone else, but keeps it in the bank for the duration of the loan. More on this later.

## Larger Business Loans

As these small businesses grow, they outgrow their local bank. Sure, they keep a few accounts at the local bank, but they get their major financing from other specialized sources. Even if the local bank is a branch of a huge international banking conglomerate, the medium-sized business will not deal with the locals for a $50 million credit line. They'll be dealing with specialists at the national headquarters.

## Commercial Real Estate Loans

This is a specialized area because the loans can become massive. Somebody put up the money for that giant regional mall near you. In order to suck in customers from a hundred-mile radius, the mall needed 75 stores. We could be talking $50 million to well over $100 million to build a big mall or skyscraper in a metropolitan area.

Even when it's only a small strip mall with a sandwich shop, shoe repair store, and a half-dozen other stores, the loan process is specialized. Bankers want to look at the income-producing capacity of those stores, and the creditworthiness of the owner or the chain.

## Consumer Loans

If you're grown up and want to buy an expensive toy, you go to the bank. There, Joe can walk out with the money for that bass boat, merely by agreeing to do three things:

1. Make the payments.
2. Allow the bass boat to be collateral. As long as he still has payments to make, he does not get *title*, or ownership of the boat.
3. Be on the hook for the full value of that loan, including interest and penalties, even if they take the boat away and sell it. Whatever value Joe owes, which the boat sale does not cover, well, he still owes it.

When times are good, this isn't a bad deal. Joe makes more money at the factory and can finance his bass boat, his 50-inch plasma TV, and any other goodies that are bigger than his neighbors have.

## Residential Real Estate

This is a massive market, valued into the trillions of dollars just in the United States alone. Because it's so large, the residential loan arena has become as standardized as a cookie cutter.

This market is also at the root of the entire financial mess the world is in right now. The mess has to do with a banking trend over many years.

When your parents bought the house you grew up in, the bank gave your parents the money for it, and kept that loan on their books. Mom and Dad made monthly payments to that bank.

Most businesses want to get bigger, and banks are no different. At the same time they're subject to that pesky "bank charter," which has all sorts of regulations.

Some of the regulations relate to the amount of loans a bank can make. That amount can be only a certain multiple of bank assets. Therefore, if a bank has $10 million in deposits, it can lend a certain amount. If it has $20 million in deposits, it can lend double that amount, as a gross generalization.

Those gray-suited bankers smile and get livelier when they can make lots of money from loan fees. But how can they make lots more loans, and get lots more fees, when they can't attract lots more deposits into their bank?

They figured out that they can pull it off if they merely "originate" the loans. They help you fill out the paperwork on the loan, and give you the money for the house. You may think you're paying back the bank over the next 30 years, but you won't be. Not long after the ink dries on that mortgage, they sell the loan to Fannie Mae, Freddie Mac, or other companies.

Your monthly check is routed from your bank to that new owner of the loan, and your local bank is completely out of the picture. Those bankers were gleeful when this practice came into fashion. They could lend money 'til the cows came home, make their loan fees from the borrowers, make more fees from selling the loans to someone else, and not have to worry about their loan-to-asset ratio getting out of whack.

You did not buy this book in order to read the history behind the current mortgage mess, so I won't bore you with the details. The important thing to remember here is that your local bank does not own the vast majority of residential mortgages it created. They've long since sold that paper.

## Auto Loans

This area is similar to residential real estate, in that the volume is very high. As a result, your fancy-dressing car dealer may seem to lend you the money for the car, but in reality does not. It's usually a giant company like General Motors Acceptance Corporation (GMAC), Ford Motor Credit, or one of a few others.

You may make payments to Ralph's Honda, or even to your bank, but neither Ralph nor your bank keeps that loan for long.

## Credit Card Debt

This is also a highly standardized area. Although credit cards seem to come in thousands of varieties, that's all window dressing. There are only a few dozen huge players in that game, like MasterCard, Visa, American Express, and the largest banks.

This is true even though your credit card may prominently feature the name of many different organizations. As with some of the other instruments I listed previously, most banks only make a fee off the credit card, and pass the main relationship onto a major national company.

## Other Loans

This isn't a course on finance, where we might veer off into discussing margin loans for buying stock, debentures for financing sports arenas, and dozens of other loan types. You can make more money than you could possibly spend in your lifetime by sticking to just a subset of the loan types I've outlined.

## Where to Start

The preceding list of loan types is by no means comprehensive. With so many types to choose from, where should you start?

Start with what you know. You're a consumer. You will be able to establish some natural rapport with other consumers who became borrowers and then delinquent borrowers. That's a great way to ease into the business.

On the other hand, I would not recommend jumping into real estate loans as your first collection effort, unless you're highly versed in the subject. You won't understand the business or the jargon.

At my company, we got quite good at consumer loans, and only afterward branched out into real estate loans and finally credit card balances.

As a consumer, you might be able to skip over real estate, and go from consumer loans to credit card portfolios. Eventually you can get into real estate and many other types of paper. You'll know when you are ready.

Now let's look at the suppliers of loan portfolios.

## Sources of Loan Portfolios

For our purposes, there are four main sources of loan portfolios:

1. The Federal Deposit Insurance Corporation (FDIC)
2. New bailout/stimulus entities
3. Loan brokers
4. Banks

Let's examine the advantages and distinctions of each source.

## Source #1: The FDIC

If you walk into most banks around the country, you cannot pass the front door without seeing a sticker on the glass nearby: In big black letters on gold, it says "FDIC."

Ever since the run on banks in the 1920s, it's been important to maintain confidence in the banking system. The government does that largely through the FDIC, which it created in 1933.

When a bank is federally chartered (and also when it's chartered in most states), the good news is consumers know their money is protected by the federal government. The FDIC's own web site says: "If you and your family have $250,000 or less in all of your deposit accounts at the same insured bank, you do not need to worry about your insurance coverage—your deposits are fully insured."

It's possible to be covered for more than $250,000, depending on the nature of the accounts you open at the bank.

In exchange for that federal backing, the bank must comply with lots of FDIC guidelines. It must maintain its books and records using strict rules for how to record every dollar of loans, investments, interest earnings, and so on.

The FDIC monitors each bank. It will watch certain banks more closely if it appears that those banks are experiencing more financial hardship than the normal ups and downs any business encounters.

On occasion, the FDIC will swoop in and take over control of a bank that suddenly reports severe financial trouble. To give you an idea of the current trends, here are the statistics for failed banks that the FDIC took over:

---

2001: 4 failed banks
2002: 11
2003: 3
2004: 4
2005: 0
2006: 0
2007: 3
2008: 25 failed banks!

---

Oh, and on just one weekend in February of 2009, four more banks went under without any big media fanfare. After all, it's getting quite common.

I already talked about the magnitude of the issue in an earlier chapter. My point here is the FDIC is a very active organization nowadays.

I have many years of experience working closely with the FDIC. In fact, remember that first $13,000 deal I did? It was the first portfolio of loans offered by the FDIC to anyone, ever.

I have found the FDIC to be a highly professional and well-run agency in the government. Now how often do you hear that?

It's important to note that the FDIC has been active with bank monitoring for 75 years. In just about every year, it's had to deal with failures. Certainly the volume in some years has been much higher than in others. When I dealt with them beginning in 1986, they were exploding in activity, and just beginning to package those loans for others to buy. Here's that chart again: Figure 4.1 illustrates FDIC activity as well as the activity of other organizations like the Resolution Trust Corporation.

Because the FDIC has had 75 years of dealing with bank crises— more or less every year—they have become very good at it. And because they've been in business throughout this period, they can

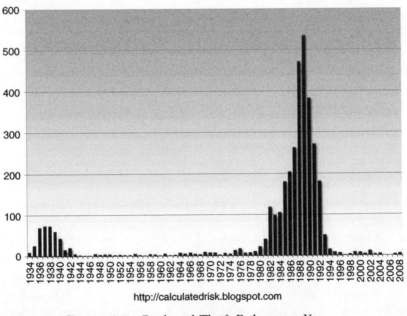

http://calculatedrisk.blogspot.com

FIGURE 4.1   Bank and Thrift Failures per Year

ramp up quickly to handle the influx of bad assets—unlike some outfits I discuss later.

## Good News and Bad News

The fact that the FDIC is quite good at what it does is something that cuts both ways.

The upside is that you will not be subjected to blundering bureaucrats who don't know what they're doing. The portfolios offered by the FDIC are thoroughly analyzed and packaged.

That's also the downside. You will get what you thought you would get—no more and no less. There will be no "diamonds in the rough."

When I first dealt with them, I had zero experience. Even though they had been in business for some decades before that point, it was a new activity for the FDIC to package loans and sell them to people like me. I found some great little gems in those portfolios—borrowers who paid much more readily than the file led me to believe they would. I do not expect that to happen with today's portfolios.

## Types of Portfolios

It's not very likely that an FDIC portfolio will contain real estate. Although the FDIC does deal with some real estate, remember that its main focus is banks. Also remember that the vast majority of bank loans for real estate are sold to other institutions. When an FDIC-insured bank fails, almost all of the assets are small business and consumer loans—Joe's bass boat, and the pizza ovens that the corner pizzeria used before it went under.

You will recall that those assets are held as collateral. You'll also recall that when the bank seizes and sells that collateral, the sale usually does not earn enough to pay back the loans entirely. Therefore the bank calculates a "deficiency balance" for the amount still owed, and tries to collect from the person who borrowed the money.

The FDIC portfolios come in many sizes, but some of them are within the reach of small investors. Again, my first portfolio of $13,000 was from the FDIC.

## FDICSales.com

A further indication that the FDIC is a well-run organization is its creation of a web site called www.FDICSales.com.

There are three ways to sell a portfolio:

1. Public outcry, where bidders participate in a public auction and shout out what they're willing to pay.
2. Sealed bid, where bidders indicate what they'll pay, but do not know what the other bidders are offering. Bidders are not even aware whether there *are* other bidders.
3. Online auction. This third option is the new kid on the block, inspired by eBay. It's a great format for all parties concerned.

   First, from the FDIC's point of view, it allows more than one round of bidding. People can bid as often as they wish, instead of just once by sealed bid.

   Second, it certainly opens up the process to many more people around the country.

   Third, it accelerates the whole process for everyone concerned. Gone are the Pony Express days of doing all this by mail, then having FDIC staff enter bids into some antiquated system by hand. Bidders enter their own bids.

Given the avalanche of assets the FDIC is seeing, it needs all the speed it can possibly get.

## FDIC Loan Sales Advisors

The actual auction process is handled for the FDIC by designated Loan Sales Advisors. No doubt the number will grow, but currently there are two such firms:

1. First Financial Network: www.firstfinancialnet.com
2. DebtX, The Debt Exchange: www.debtx.com

To quote the FDIC:

Each advisor has the ability to offer both electronic due diligence on their website and hard copy due diligence. Each of their websites has an internet bid platform where bids on FDIC loan sales will be submitted.

If you are interested in participating in a loan sale offering, you are recommended to contact each of the loan sale advisors and request an account on their web site. Each advisor has their own requirements for granting access to their site. You are encouraged to make application so you will receive notice of any FDIC loan sale offering.

By registering at these sites, you can be alerted by email of new portfolios.

It's a good idea to register at the FDIC main site also, in order to be alerted to other news, such as the appointment of new Loan Sales Advisors.

## Who Cannot Play

I told you the FDIC has become quite sophisticated and efficient over time. That knowledge is reflected in the long list of entities that are *not* eligible to buy loan portfolios, including:

- FDIC employees
- Delinquent Obligors (i.e., the very people whose loans are in default)
- Officers or directors of failed institutions
- People convicted of certain crimes
- People who have used tactics that, although not criminal, are not acceptable to the FDIC

## Source #2: New Bailout/Stimulus Entities

This is truly the trillion-pound gorilla of the bad loan business. That's because a huge focus of the current government plan is on programs that will handle these loans.

It's so big that it will change the law of supply and demand in this country. In a minute I'll explain how, but let's first look at what these programs do.

As you know, the FDIC never was mothballed, because there have been bank failures almost every year. In 1989, however, the Resolution Trust Corporation came into being to handle the savings and loan crisis.

The focus of RTC was to dispose of real estate assets those savings and loans had accumulated before they went four-legs-in-the-air, so to speak.

Like a supernova, the RTC went from nothing to an enormous entity in a very short time—then faded back to nothingness. In 1995, the RTC ceased to exist and was absorbed into the FDIC. During its six-year run, RTC handled the assets of 747 entities, with assets totaling $394 billion.

Let's see: Six years to handle $394 billion, versus my estimate of two years now to handle more than $1 trillion. And that's just the dollars we've heard about so far.

Needless to say, the government has been hard at work, brushing the mothballs off its entire RTC structure.

This is not a theory of mine. As I said in Chapter 1, I was minding my own business, happily pedaling away on my stationary bike, when Neel Kashkari appeared on television. He is a 35-year-old former aerospace engineer. He then became Interim Assistant Secretary of the Treasury for Financial Stability.

Maybe it does take a rocket scientist to be in that position after all.

Anyway, as I was pedaling, Mr. Kashkari began to outline the main principles under which the Troubled Asset Resolution

Program (TARP) would operate. By the third of the seven principles, I was saying them out loud before he did.

Dear reader, TARP looked like a bigger, bolder version of RTC all over again.

Just as the FDIC's assets will primarily be consumer and small business loans, the assets the government will deal with will primarily be those of banks, which in turn will disgorge loans of all types, including consumer loans, small business loans, and so on.

In case you're wondering: Even though loans are usually considered a liability to the borrower, they're an asset to the lender. They are an income-producing entity—until some of them reach the point of being uncollectable. They're still called assets, though.

## Good News and Bad News

My company was a major dealer of loans we got from RTC and repackaged to other buyers, to the tune of over $6 billion in assets. I saw RTC up close and personal, as they say.

The good news is that the RTC worked pretty well for a brand-new organization. There were ups and downs, but for the most part it disposed of the assets in an efficient manner.

I'm guessing that right at this moment, there's an army of bureaucrats combing through millions of pages of RTC records, manuals, court cases, memos, and edicts. That army is charged with updating the entire system just as fast as humanly possible.

The bad news is the RTC engine has been stone-cold for 13 years. That means most of the brains that ran RTC have had 13 years to find and settle into other jobs. No doubt the most senior people have retired.

The staff that will be hired to run the current government entities will be new. Kind of like the CIA scouring the country for Arabic-speaking experts after 9/11.

These old structures with new acronyms will create the biggest asset jumble of any loan supplier.

There's a greater likelihood that banks that receive government funds will sell loan portfolios containing both unusual problems and gems. They're just not going to have the same luxury of time and experience, relatively speaking, that the FDIC can apply to its loan portfolios.

The new government programs will be dealing with banks involved with those bad Fannie Mae and Freddie Mac assets we've heard so much about: You know, the subprime borrowers who never should have bought big houses in the first place.

Because banks infused with government funds will be so exceedingly busy, it's likely that their loan packages will be larger than what's over at the FDIC and other suppliers.

## Objection

Bill, now you're making me concerned. I feel like by the time I get into this opportunity, it will all be picked over by the Big Boys. Besides, you know I can't invest in a big package of loans.

How wrong you are! Sure, most people will look at the facts the way you just did. But remember what hockey legend Wayne Gretzky said:

A good hockey player plays where the puck is. A great hockey player plays where the puck is going to be.

I mentioned earlier that banks naturally want to get bigger, so they sell their residential mortgages and car loans. They do that in order to make fees and not be prevented from making still more loans.

Well, the same is true with loan collection companies. A few of them have been around ever since the RTC was in its heyday. Two things are happening with these suppliers.

## The Big Boys

First, many of the most sophisticated companies are no longer focusing on this business. Let's see, in 2008 alone Merrill Lynch was bought, Bear Stearns was restructured, and Lehman Brothers went under.

For the most part, Chase Manhattan, Citigroup, and Bank of America are not big into this business. If they do decide to get big, they'll be building from scratch. A few other major firms like Morgan Stanley and Goldman Sachs may participate, but we'll see.

Even if all the firms just named jumped in at the same time, I'm telling you they would be a drop in the bucket. Take the nimblest of players, Warren Buffett. In September 2008, he injected $5 billion into Goldman Sachs. Let's say the Oracle of Omaha, as they call Buffett, sees this opportunity in bad debt and decides to dump in an amount that's triple the size of his investment in Goldman. Warren writes a check for 15 billion smackers!

Big deal. He's about the biggest player around, with the most cash, and even Buffett now has taken care of only $15 billion of a $1 trillion-plus immediate problem. Hooray, only $985 billion to go. Not counting credit card debt, auto debt, consumer loan debt, and the list goes on and on.

Are you beginning to grasp the magnitude of the problem/opportunity before us?

## The Smaller Fry

Second, there are the smaller players. Some of them have stayed in the business, and are licking their chops at what they see about to happen. What are they likely to do? Get bigger, of course. They'll start gearing up to take big slugs of government-induced paper, in order to make hay while the sun shines.

What will that do to the market? That giant sucking sound you hear will be the existing players moving up into bigger offices, leaving the smaller portfolios for you to take advantage of.

Stated another way, even if you never had any intention of buying a big portfolio, other people will do so, and everyone will move up the ladder one or two rungs, leaving plenty of room for you to hop on that ladder.

When I got into this business with that first FDIC portfolio in 1986, it took four years before I saw any significant competition. This time around, the opportunity is upon us now, and—as I said earlier— I estimate it to be a two-year window of maximum opportunity.

Big, paper-pushing organizations are going to miss the boat. You have an advantage in that you're a small shop. You do not have 13 layers of committees that must prepare mission statements, memorandums of understanding, requests for proposal, joint venture agreements, operating agreements, and countless other papers in order to act. You can act with literally a handful of pages of documents, which I describe in a later chapter.

This time around, the small and nimble will enjoy a disproportionate amount of the benefits.

## Special Groups

I briefly mentioned this in an earlier chapter. When RTC was created, it had a mandate to work with the small investor and other special groups, and not just sell big portfolios to the Big Boys.

That same opportunity has carried over to the present. Even in the earliest documents relating to how the program will work, they've explicitly mentioned that alphabet soup of:

- VOSBs (Veteran-Owned Small Businesses)
- SDVOSBs (Service-Disabled Veteran-Owned Small Businesses)
- HUBZone (Small Business Concerns)

- SDBs (Certified Small Business Concerns Owned and Controlled by Socially and Economically Disadvantaged Individuals)
- WOSBs (Women- and Minority-Owned Businesses)

I bet they won't be able to help themselves and will cook up some more alphabet soup categories before the dust settles.

Do I know precisely how all these groups will participate? No. No one does. I do know that there will be a big effort to show that this opportunity is extended to as much of the American population as possible.

The FDIC never recognized these special categories, as far as I am aware. But with the new government programs, those special groups—coupled with that space at the bottom rungs of the size ladder—spell one thing: extraordinary opportunity for you.

## Source #3: Brokers

I am not referring to Wall Street stockbrokers, but instead specialists in the buying and selling of non-performing paper.

Brokers make their money in two ways. They might act as *principal* or dealer, where they buy big packages at wholesale prices, then bust up the packages for other buyers, selling them at retail prices.

Others are simply brokers who pass on the deals with no markup, but they take a fee on each deal. One compensation method is not better or worse than the other; it depends on the pricing of the deal you're looking at.

On the one hand, you'll pay more through a broker than if you went directly to the portfolio source. On the other hand, you benefit in several ways:

- You may not qualify to buy directly from the source, but the broker does. Therefore, you could see deals you otherwise would not have access to.

- The broker may package a portfolio more precisely, so you get and pay for just the kind of loans you want. For instance, they may be located in your target state or city, or they may be of a certain loan type you prefer.

- Once you get into this business, you may get hooked, and want to do many more deals. I know I did. In that case, you want multiple sources for deals. Brokers can become your "bird dogs," locating new portfolios of the type they know you like.

## National Loan Exchange

My company dealt for years with NLEX, as the National Loan Exchange is known (www.nlex.com). We were buyers of portfolios from NLEX as well as sellers to them.

David Ludwig, the head of NLEX, got into the business a few years after I did. As with most industries, you can find good guys and bad guys. Dave is one of the Good Guys.

NLEX does not buy, mark up, and sell loan portfolios; it acts simply as a broker, charging a fee.

In case you wonder if all the best deals are somehow snapped up before small investors ever see them, there's a remedy for that: The auctions stay open for a period of time, so everyone has a chance to bid on them.

You have an opportunity to examine the loan portfolio before bidding, so you can formulate your offering and maximum price. I discuss in a later chapter at some length how to examine the portfolio.

NLEX offers packages for small investors, all the way up to very large ones for the big players. Over the years the packaging has become more sophisticated. In the 1990s you would have seen a blend of various assets from one bank. Today it's possible to specify assets by state or other criteria.

NLEX does not finance your purchase of a portfolio. You'll have to get financing elsewhere. I discuss that process in a later chapter.

There are many other brokers, and each has a specialty. One broker, Charge-Off Clearinghouse (www.chargeoffclearinghouse .com) has small portfolios at very low cost, which is good news to beginning investors. You're able to practice and get good with a small portfolio. The flip side is that some of the loans can be quite old—I've seen some that were as old as eight years.

With loans that old, part of your portfolio research would involve knowing what the statute of limitations is in the states where those borrowers live. Each state has rules about how long a delinquent loan can be pursued.

> Bill, I've always wondered something about companies that sell opportunities to other companies and individuals: If the opportunity is so good, why aren't they keeping it for themselves?

The answer has to do with what's called a "satiated situation." Let's say you're that company which sells opportunities to others, and you're starting out in business. You might very well do some cherry-picking of the best deals for yourself. At least, you might grab the deals that are best for you, in that they relate to the kind of loans you've personally had the most success with.

You can only do so much cherry-picking before you run out of resources to take all the good ones you see. If you were buying and selling some very rare antiques, I suppose you could corner the market.

In our case, we're talking defaulted loans. I've already pointed out that $1 trillion or so is merely a single piece of the puzzle. When all is said and done, this bad-debt puzzle will total multiple trillions of dollars. And you're worried that one, or 10, or even 1,000 players will grab all the good stuff?

Here's another perspective: Imagine one of those grain elevators in the Midwest. The ones that hold like a million bushels of wheat. Should the Wonder Bread Bakery be concerned that the grain elevator operator will grab all the best wheat for himself and give Wonder Bread the lousy wheat?

The grain elevator operator is in the business of storing grain. Wonder Bread bakes it. The loan packager is in the business of packaging loans for a fee. You are in the business of recovering money from those loans.

By the way, there are about as many loans out there as there is grain in that elevator.

## In the Next Chapter

We've just looked at the types of loans you may run across, and three sources for those deals. In the next chapter we will look at another very special and potentially fruitful source.

# How to Find Good Deals, Part Two

I'm a student of human nature. I believe most people don't even bother to better themselves. A certain number will buy a book like this, but never get around to reading it. I'm impressed that here you are, reading all the way into Chapter 5. You're likely to make it in this business because you have enough motivation and discipline to take action.

I'm going to reward your action by handing you an unbelievably good source for loan deals. It's none other than your local bank.

## Source #4: Your Local Bank

That's right: Perhaps the very best way to get filthy rich in this business is to start with the outfit that's been right under your nose, in your hometown, all this time.

Remember our discussion in the last chapter about all the loans a bank makes? Let's look at what happens at a typical but imaginary bank by the name of First National Bank.

Frank Smith is the president. It's not a large bank with a large staff, so Frank's heavily involved in all important decisions.

First National offers all the same services that any good bank does. Its single-family residential loans are sold to Fannie Mae or another outfit in exchange for fees. The car loans are sold to GMAC or someone else in exchange for fees. Everything else pretty much stays with the bank.

Because First National is about as good as every other bank, most of its loans will be repaid on time. When some borrowers fall behind, they'll get mail notices and then phone calls. With increasing urgency, the bank will ask for the money and explain the consequences of not paying. Those efforts will be successful with some borrowers, and not with others.

The unsuccessful efforts will result in repossession of the assets, and any money still remaining to be paid will become a *deficiency balance*. First National writes the value of those assets down to zero, as regulations require. It then packages up similarly late loans and sends them to a collection agency.

No doubt the agency will collect on some loans, for which it is paid a fee. It returns the rest to the bank, which may try with a second or even third agency. Eventually the bank stops all efforts on those loans that have resisted every collection effort.

Important point: The state "statute of limitations" laws vary in the extreme. This is the window during which the law allows First National or any of its agents (like collection agencies) to try to collect from a borrower.

For written contracts, it is as short as three years in Maryland and New Hampshire. However, the statute is *fifteen years* in Kentucky and Ohio! In most states it's around six years. Most banks will cease all collection efforts long before the statute runs out. In other words, the loans are still collectable for quite some time after all collection efforts cease.

Frank's pretty experienced as bank president, so he works hard to extract all dollars from the delinquent borrowers. Even so, at some point he must face facts and stop wasting time and money on a lost cause. After all, he has newer delinquent loans to chase. He directs his collections department to bundle up six months of old, bad loans and store them away in the warehouse. At some point after the statute of limitations runs out, they'll send those papers to the shredder.

First National Bank is doing okay financially—not great, but not about to fail. Frank wakes up every morning thinking about how he can trim overhead and make more fees from loans. He'd like to spend more time and money on advertising, but can't. He'd like to spend more time and money on the collection of old debts, but he can't do that either. It's a matter of juggling his best opportunities for profit, and putting other projects on the back burner. That's just business.

I've just described to you what's known in business as an "inefficient market." Frank's bank is as efficient as the next bank, but everything is not tied into some central national database.

Contrast that situation with what happens when you want to buy stock in IBM. Whether you're at home in front of your computer, or standing in Times Square watching the stock ticker, the price of one share of IBM stock is precisely the same at the same moment. Economists call that a highly efficient market. Everyone has pretty much the same information about the IBM company, and everyone buys that stock on the New York Stock Exchange.

A somewhat less efficient market is a Big Mac at McDonald's. If you roll up to the drive-through window here in Tulsa, it might cost you $2.75 on Sunday. If you buy it at the McDonald's in Chicago O'Hare Airport on that same Sunday, it will cost $4.50. At the McDonald's concession area during that same Super Bowl Sunday, that same burger will run you $5.75. McDonald's wisely varies its Big Mac price largely according to demand at the time, among other factors.

At the most "inefficient" end of the market you have the local antiques store. They have lots of junk and a few nice pieces. In the days before eBay, they only drew customers from so many miles around the store. Some buyers pay far too much for what they think is a beautiful chest of drawers, and other people walk away with amazing bargains. I know of one woman who bought a plain-looking amber necklace. When she had it appraised, she was offered $80,000 for the necklace: In microscopic print on each bead it said "From Napoleon to Josephine."

Well, Frank's file room in the basement of First National Bank is much closer to the antique store than it is to Times Square. And one other thing: Zero customers are shopping in Frank's basement. He regards the merchandise as worthless, and soon to be destroyed.

In you walk with an offer. You want to examine his dead-loan file and pay him money.

Frank's never heard of such a thing because no one's ever offered him money for a worthless asset before.

Does he suddenly think that those files contain hidden treasures of amber? No. He's been in the banking business for 21 years, and he knows his borrowers. The basement is his boneyard of nonpaying borrowers who fleeced First National Bank out of funds, for one reason or another.

And lest Frank think that he just overlooked something, he had three separate collection agencies try their best with these loans. His basement contains the toxic sludge that remained after all valuable elements had been skimmed off.

No, Frank figures you must be some kind of nut. The thing is, though, that you don't talk like a nut. You actually seem pretty professional. Furthermore, you came armed with quite an impressive document that describes what you propose to do.

In my experience in actually taking the above approach, I'll tell you what goes through Frank's mind:

- This guy in front of me has a professional presentation.
- I have utterly worthless assets sitting in my basement, making me no money. In fact, they're costing me storage space until I can destroy them.

- All the guy wants is access to worthless files, in order to make me an offer.

- It's not like he can be a "mole" for the bank across town, because they're worthless files of deadbeat borrowers. I wish my competition had more of those type customers!

- I'm in the business of earning fees. I might get a fee from this guy, for no work on my part. That money goes straight to the bottom line.

I'm telling you: For a beginning borrower, this Option #4 with the local bank is hands-down the very best way to break into this business.

I'm not finished with the good news yet: Stick with me, and I'll show you how that bank is likely to give you 100 percent financing for the loan portfolio!

Now aren't you glad you kept reading all the way up to Chapter 5?


## Do These Things and You're Sure to Fail

I can see it now: I get someone so whipped up into a lather that he hops in his car and drives down to the local bank.

He walks in and says, "I need to see the bank president."

"Well, sir, do you have an appointment?"

"No, but I want to buy all your bad loans. Now can I talk with the president?"

Let me spare you the further dialogue, because I know the outcome. He will fail. No matter how badly Frank wants more fees, and no matter how dusty those files are in the basement, you *cannot* just barge in the front door and start your pitch. So don't waste your time.

The other great way to fail is to pick the wrong bank. You need a *local* bank, not a *local* branch of a *national* bank.

The mega banks that advertise during the Olympics are not your target market. It doesn't matter that the bank has a branch in your community with nice, friendly, locally grown tellers: They're so tightly controlled by headquarters that the branch manager can't move a potted plant without permission.

You should look for a bank with only a local presence. It may have a few branches in town, or even in multiple surrounding towns. If it's doing any advertising, it will consist of pictures of piggybanks in the newspaper, or perhaps a TV commercial during a local sports show.

These banks are owned and controlled by people in your town. They don't make decisions by committee. Frank decides. Occasionally the board of directors must meet to approve larger matters. In that case Frank has a vote, and so does Mary (Frank's sister-in-law), Ralph (Frank's cousin), Bob (local attorney), and a couple other upstanding citizens in town.

Of the more than 8,000 banks in America, I just described the majority of them. Sure, some of the Big Boys have thousands of branches in many cities. Ignore those, and focus on the truly local banks.

By the way, you'll have no competition. The really smart players in this business are most definitely not approaching local banks, one at a time. As I said earlier, they're salivating at the prospect of doing the Deal of Their Lifetime with the feds. Unlike just about every other tested-and-proven great business opportunity on the face of this planet, *you will have no competition.*

## How to Approach Your Local Bank

The process is not difficult, but it *is* a specific process. Do not get creative without first using my process.

It's no different from learning to bake your first cake: Just bake the cake in the recipe. If you get good at that, then by all means branch out and try variations. But if you've never baked a cake, get a recipe—and if you don't follow the recipe directions in the first place—you're an idiot.

Follow my steps. You can thank me later.

## Make an Appointment

I've already established that you do not want to walk into a bank and ask to see the person in charge. The *only way* you should walk into a bank is when you have an appointment to see that person.

But Bill, I don't know anyone at the bank.

Okay. Do you have an accountant?

Well, no.

Do you have a lawyer?

Yes, I do.

That's where you start, then. I can assure you that your lawyer or accountant knows lots of people in town. In the 1990s, a playwright named John Guare popularized an old concept called *six degrees of separation*.

The idea is that anyone on the planet is separated from anyone else by at most six people: Your friend knows the mayor, who's met the senator, who knows the president, who knows the pope. That kind of thing.

If you have a competent lawyer—somebody from a decent-sized firm in your local community—she would certainly know presidents of local banks and probably have done business with them. It isn't always true but it will be likely. If the lawyer is part of a multi-person firm, rather than a sole practitioner, the firm might even represent the bank or have a member on the board of the bank. At least they belong to the only country club in town, along with some bank people.

Therefore, you ask your lawyer (or accountant, plumber, doctor, or veterinarian) for an introduction.

### But Bill, I don't know anyone in town!

Then remedy that. You want to be in business, right? That's why you're reading this book in the first place, right? Then find a competent lawyer and accountant.

It need not be the most expensive person in town. Do not go after the bargain-basement person, either. Just ask around until you locate an experienced person with a good reputation. It really is a condition of doing business, and it won't cost much.

### How do I ask this person for an introduction?

It depends on your situation. If you do a decent amount of business with that lawyer, then call her up and ask to see her for a few minutes. Do not make your presentation over the phone. You want to go in and see her.

If you have that relatively good relationship, then you can grab a few minutes and it won't cost you anything. You're the client, remember?

On the other hand, let's say you have only a new or infrequent relationship with your lawyer. You may then have to schedule a brief consultation. That's right, you may have to pay a few dollars to get on your lawyer's calendar.

So what. Consider it a very smart investment.

In your meeting, say this:

Mary, I've been working on a concept I'm very excited about. It's something that I think could be a win/win for the First National Bank, and also for me.

As you of course know, the news is filled with talk about the government bailout, and all the bad loans that banks have made to consumers. Well, that got me thinking. I happen to know a guy who literally made over a billion dollars by using some courteous and polite—but very effective—ways of collecting on debts when the usual strong-arm debt collection techniques didn't work.

I have a business proposal that I want to present to First National Bank. I have it right here. It involves reviewing the loans that the bank has already written off down to zero value. I think I know a way to have some of those loans pay off after all. That will mean *found money* to the bank, and some money to me, too.

Do you know anyone over at the bank?

The chances are excellent that she does. If she doesn't, that tells you something about your lawyer. In that case, ask if she knows someone who would know, and whether she knows the heads of any other local banks.

Let's assume she does know someone at the bank. Then say:

> I don't want to bore you with all the details of what I have in mind. But I can tell you that I only want five minutes of that person's time at the bank. What did you say his name was? Frank Smith?
>
> By the way, I'm not asking you to come along, or even to vouch for the plan. I'll do all that myself. However, if you wanted to tell him later that I was a nice guy, well, that wouldn't hurt my feelings any. How would you feel about giving him a call now, at least starting as an introduction so that I can go over to meet with Mr. Smith to present my plan?

Then you sit there and shut up. Do not keep blabbering on. Mary is on the hot seat, being asked by you—her paying client—for a very standard and simple introduction. Don't take her off the hot seat by continuing to speak.

Notice that you're asking Mary to make the call *while you're present*. That's the best of all worlds. Naturally, you'll settle for whatever you have to settle for, but try to have the call made then and there. It's as simple as saying:

> Would you mind giving your buddy Frank a call for me? I'd really appreciate that and I'll call him later to make the appointment. But if you were to do that for me, I'd really appreciate that.

At that point, she's almost gotta pick up the phone.

> Hey Frank, I've got Bill Bartmann here in front of me and Bill's got a business plan he wants to pitch to you, so I'm calling to make this introduction. Yeah Bill's one of my clients. Yeah, I've known Bill for almost a year now.

He's got this really intriguing idea that, quite frankly, I think you might find interesting, but I promised him I wouldn't tell you about it. I'm gonna let him tell you about it. Would you have five minutes for him?

If you're sitting there, it becomes way harder for Mary to forget to call, or forget what the call was about, or mumble something about "I got this guy who's pestering me to call you. It sounds like a crazy idea, but would you just talk to the guy for five minutes?" Instead, she'll say something nice because you're staring at her.

You just got a wonderful introduction and now Frank is going to give you five minutes. He'll probably even pay attention for five minutes, not because he likes you, but because now there is somebody else invested in the game (Mary).

You've just gained two things:

1. You're finding out who's the right person to talk to instead of the wrong person. If you blundered into to the bank and got a "No," it would be just about impossible to get over that "No." Ever.
2. When you walk into that bank, it will be with an appointment to see Frank, and your head will be held high.

You'll probably get the phone call made in your presence. Worst case scenario is your lawyer saying, "I'm running late for a court appointment right now, but yeah, sure, I'll be happy to call this afternoon."

Wait a couple of days and check with your lawyer: "Say, Mary, were you able to make the call over to Frank at First National Bank?"

If it happened, then great. If it hasn't happened, say, "Could you please just give me a quick call to know when it's okay for me to call Mr. Smith at the bank to make my appointment?"

Once you hear that the call has been made, waste no time calling the bank. Call a few hours later.

You are calling Frank Smith's office and will most likely get Susie, who is Frank's secretary. Remember that you're not a stranger at this point:

---

**Susie:** Mr. Smith's office.

**You:** Hi, my name is Bill Bartmann. May I please speak with Mr. Smith?

**Susie:** May I tell him what it's regarding?

**You:** Yes, Mr. Smith is expecting my call. We have a mutual friend by the name of Mary Jones. Mary recently spoke with Mr. Smith about a revenue opportunity I have for your bank, and Mr. Smith said he'd be willing to see me.

---

If Mr. Smith is not in, she'll tell you that. In that case, ask Susie for a time that's available for Mr. Smith to see you. If he keeps his own calendar, or if she just puts you through to him, then say:

> Hi, Mr. Smith, my name is Bill Bartmann. Mary Jones said that you'd be willing to visit with me for a few minutes. When would that be convenient for you?

You are now the proud owner of five minutes on Frank Smith's calendar at First National Bank.

> Okay. But what if I get Mr. Smith on the phone, and he wants to grill me on the spot about the opportunity?

That's unlikely, but here's what you do:

**Mr. Smith:** Mr. Bartmann, why don't you just tell me what your idea is right now?

**You:** Certainly, I'd be happy to do that. I have an opportunity to put some capital back on your balance sheet by purchasing from your institution some of the loans that you are no longer collecting on.

 I know that's a strange concept and it's probably one that hasn't been presented to you previously, but I hope that my relationship with Mary tells you that I'm someone of some substance and I can, in fact, execute on this deal. I'd love to have five minutes to spend with you.

**Mr. Smith:** Is loan purchasing something that you've done before, Mr. Bartmann?

**You:** Well, actually it is not something that I've done, but something that has been going on out there for a very long time, as you know. During that five minutes that I'm asking you for, I'll be able to explain all of this.

 In fact, I have it written down and well-thought-out and prepared. Again, I'm only going to ask for five minutes of your time.

---

If Mr. Smith says "no" now to your simple request, jettison him.

You must have a certain attitude here: On the one hand, don't be condescending and talk down to Mr. Smith, as if you can collect on loans that he could not. On the other hand, don't come across as begging. You're not doing Mr. Smith a favor, and he's not doing you one. It's a business proposition.

If he's not receptive after a very professional introduction, then you need one word in your head: "Next." You move on to other banks. Remember, you only need one bank to say "yes" every now and then.

You might get somebody who says: "Well, just tell me what the proposal is and how much it would pay. What kind of loans do you want?" If he takes you down that path, you're already beginning to lose.

That's when you need to say, "Sir, I'll give you all the details when we meet. If I may have five minutes, I would really appreciate that."

## A Good Strategy

Here's a great but optional strategy for you to think about using: Go out of town to role play.

We did that very thing when we had grown large enough that we were in the market to borrow tens of millions of dollars. We knew we would soon visit some of the Big Boys in the investment banking community, but we wanted more practice first.

We called up regional investment banking companies—people we didn't want to do business with. We just knew they would not be a good fit when we got big, but we "went to school on them," as they say. We set up meetings and pitched. Every time they said "no" to us we tried to deduce or ask why they responded that way. We then made sure the next time we pitched, the new people heard it differently. We covered that objection and tuned up our presentation.

Eventually our presentation was so good, we could go anywhere we wanted on Wall Street. That didn't happen by accident. It was a strategy.

> But Bill, if I go out of town, now I really don't know any lawyer or accountant to help me out.

I won't kid you: It's going to be a bit more difficult. You now don't have the semi-warm introduction by your lawyer, and you're pretty much down to cold calling. It's the same thing you'd have to do in your local community if you truly didn't know anyone.

What you do is call the switchboard of the bank and ask who the president is. They will tell you; they know. You say, "Oh, thank you very much" and hang up.

Wait an hour or so, and call back. This time, ask for him by name. You'll get his secretary and you're off to the races.

---

**Secretary:** Mr. Taylor's office.

**You:** Hi, my name is Bill Bartmann. I would like to meet with Mr. Taylor and I want to be honest with you. Mr. Taylor doesn't know me.

    I haven't met him yet, but I really only need five minutes, and this is what I want to talk to him about: It is an opportunity where I can put some capital back into his bank.

    Would you see if that's something that he would be willing to visit with me about?

**Secretary:** Mr. Taylor is a very busy man and his calendar is filled up long into the future. If you'd like, you could send him something.

**You:** Okay. May I have your full mailing address?

---

If that's the best I can get, I'm going to play their game. I hate it. I don't want to mail anything; I want to show up. But if I am getting blocked by the gatekeeper, something is better than nothing. A chance is better than no chance.

    Try to read the person on the phone, and don't give up too easily. If I got the above response, I might say:

> Well, this is a bit of a detailed story, but I can tell you that my proposal has to do with infusing capital into Community Bank. I hope that is adequate to convey to Mr. Taylor. If he has an interest in that, then I think we can go to the next step. Would that be okay?

    Think about the secretary's position now: You don't sound like an office supply salesman. You're using words like "infusing capital." Is she going to make a decision for the bank to turn you away? I don't think so, at least in most cases. She won't be happy that you didn't tell her more, but you have told her something that sounds serious.

She's thinking: "I don't want to be the secretary who blew an opportunity. If Mr. Taylor later found out that I kept you out, I might lose my job. I'm going to let Mr. Taylor make this decision."

She then walks in and says, "Hey, Mr. Taylor, I had some guy saying something about infusing capital into Community Bank. I'm sorry, but he didn't share much more than that. He left his telephone number."

Something new will happen next:

- Either the secretary will call you back with more specific questions from Mr. Taylor; or
- Mr. Taylor might call you.

Either way, you then pretty much say the same thing I told you to say to Frank Smith at First National. You add: "May I have five minutes of your time? I promise you it will be exactly 300 seconds. Not 301, not 299, but 300 seconds. You give me five minutes of your time and I promise to be out of there in 300 seconds."

That's intriguing. If you work this plan the way I've laid it out for you, sooner or later you'll be on the calendar of a honcho at a local bank.

## Dealing with a Junior Person

You might not luck out and get right to the bank president. At times, the best you'll do is get in to see the assistant vice president, so that's what you do.

When you're talking with that person, be careful to pitch in the same way that you would pitch the president. Why? Because you want this person repeating your story to the president in the manner you would have pitched the president.

If the assistant vice president didn't hear the real pitch—if you "dumbed it down" for him, he won't be delivering your presidential pitch to the president.

The next thing you must do is make several copies of your written presentation and hand them to the junior person. (We will go into the presentation later.) Do not rely on the bank to make copies of your presentation! They'll reproduce it crooked using some grainy, wheezing copying machine in the corner.

No, you want crisp, clean copies on nice stationery. Giving the assistant vice president three or four copies of this two-page business plan will speak volumes about you. It tells him you understand his role in this organization. It acknowledges that there is somebody upstairs, and yes, he would have had to make copies for the people upstairs, and you just saved him the time and trouble.

Again, you use the same pitch, but you subtly imply that we know he's going to have to bring it to others. After the regular pitch, you add, "I hope that whoever gets to decide these kinds of things will think this is something that really makes sense for your bank."

## Creating Your Business Plan

Don't even consider buying a loan portfolio from your local bank without a business plan.

Keep in mind that the FDIC, TARP, and loan brokers will have already packaged the portfolios. Their concerns are mainly the color of your money, though you must meet a few other requirements.

In the case of First National Bank, no "portfolio" exists. There's only a brown file box (or 15 of them) with "Charge-Offs—Destroy After May 2015" written on the side.

That's why your chances are so good at the bank: No one's competing with you, and you're saying there's buried treasure in their basement, when they thought only useless papers were down there.

Most people don't take any action at all. Of the small minority that do, most shoot from the hip. They have merely an "idea." Well, that's not a plan, and it's not sufficient when talking with Frank Smith.

The business plan need not be long. It just has to be long enough to:

- Show that you approach things professionally.
- Indicate that you have a specific approach in mind when you review the files, formulate a bid, and commence collections.
- Demonstrate that you're methodical and think clearly.
- Answer obvious objections.

## Structure of the Business Plan

Go to the office supply store and get some nice, heavy paper. You'll have lots of choices. Don't get splashy; just pick up the stuff that's labeled for business presentations.

You'll need to use a word-processing program and decent printer. Again, the goal is not to be flashy, but to look crisp and clean. They should not remember anything about the document except the content and a general feeling of being impressed. To the extent that the format or physical properties stand out—either crappy or over-the-top with leather binding and such—you are now distracting from your message.

The business plan can be as short as a couple of pages. They're not expecting anything because this whole proposal will come as news to them. You're in a great position of not competing with other, bigger players. Therefore, simply worry about getting your message across clearly, however many or few words that takes.

### Cover
On the cover, put the name of the bank in relatively big letters, as in "Non-Performing Loan Purchase Proposal for First National Bank." Your name should go lower on the cover, in smaller letters. It can be

your company name or just your own name if you don't have a company.

Do not put the name of Frank Smith or any other contact on the cover. You don't know where this will be circulated, and you want it to look like it's intended for any decision-maker within the bank. Here are the main sections, and what to cover within each section:

### Executive Summary
Simply write out the five-minute proposal here, and then edit it to sound like a written document, and not a verbal pitch. You can end the section by setting up the reader to expect the sections that follow.

### Portfolio Analysis
Once we cover due diligence in a later chapter, you'll have plenty to list in this section. It need only be a few paragraphs discussing that your review will cover many aspects of loan quality and status, including . . . (then you list a number of bullet points here).

### Formulation of Bid
You will speak in general terms about the fact that you do not make vague guesses about the entire portfolio; instead, you examine each loan history in detail. You then apply the analysis factors to the loan, and formulate a score for that loan.

You then combine all those scores for the entire portfolio. You go on to state that there is a certain unknown factor within each loan. For example, whether the borrower has since moved, declared bankruptcy, changed phone numbers, and so on. Therefore you will apply an uncertainty factor that simply reflects the reality of loans that are both old and—up to this point—uncollectable.

### Collections Strategy
This is a brief description of what is detailed more fully in a later chapter—the exact process you will take to contact the borrowers and collect from them.

This is a very important section, because it addresses the only major objection the bank could have: "How do we know you will not browbeat our borrowers and generate bad publicity for our bank?"

Do not raise the question in quite those words. Instead, make it clear that your efforts will involve not the "strong-arm" method, but the "soft-arm" method. Explain that you will be able to extend payment plans longer than the bank could afford to do.

### Optional Section: Company Description

If you have an existing company that supports your image with the bank, then by all means mention it briefly. You might be a consultant or have worked for years in financial services.

Leave this section out, though, if you run a motor oil recycling plant.

### Optional Section: Funding

You are most likely going to be returning to this bank to ask Mr. Smith to finance the very portfolio you want to buy from him.

This is an optional section, because if you have financing from somewhere else, then it's a plus to mention it here. If you instead plan to ask Mr. Smith to finance the portfolio, do not mention that plan!

You want Mr. Smith first to agree to sell you the portfolio. Then, when he's already mentally booking those extra profits, you can raise the possibility of his financing the purchase.

In your later document—the loan proposal—you will raise this topic. Not before then.

## Preparing for Your Five-Minute Pitch

Back to the appointment you've secured at the bank. You're going to deliver a powerful and effective pitch literally in the space of 300 seconds. I want you to have two thoughts in mind as you prepare:

1. On the one hand, it's an important presentation and you should not take it casually.

2. On the other hand, I don't want to stress you out and have you become so nervous that you worry about messing up—which often has the effect of messing you up.

There's a solution: You must prepare for the presentation diligently, but you can relax because nothing huge is riding on any one presentation. Will you blow it occasionally? Sure. Are there plenty of other banks around? Absolutely.

The way to prepare is first to get the entire presentation down on paper. Then practice it many times before you ever use it on a banker.

I don't care if we're talking about giving a speech, pitching a banker, hitting a golf ball, or shooting baskets—practice is the mark of a professional, and you definitely want to come across as such a person.

The script is only five minutes long. You should be able to memorize it by doing it out loud over and over again. You don't need to have every single word perfectly in place, and you certainly should not sound like you're reciting the Pledge of Allegiance. But you don't want to leave any concepts out, either.

Try to get your practice at least on audio, and preferably on video. Practice delivering it to a human listener if possible, but to your dog if necessary. Video is great because you'll see things you swore you didn't do. Maybe it's sticking your hands in your pockets, or shifting your feet back and forth. I can promise you that your 20th video will be far superior to your first.

Another reason to relax is you'll have your business plan presentation in hand, and you'll be going through the points in it. They will serve as your cue cards.

What words you actually say when you get there aren't nearly as important as how you say them. If you're comfortable with yourself, your presentation, and ability to give this five-minute presenta-tion—even though you will be scared to death—that's okay. The words *will* come because you practiced it enough.

Please understand that there are no magic words. This is not a voodoo incantation—if you get it wrong, your cousin won't turn into a toad. Just be prepared, enthusiastic, and sincere. As long as you say most of what it is you've written down, you'll do great. Remember that you will be leaving it all with him anyhow, in the form of the written business plan. Even if you didn't say it all perfectly, he will have it.

## Your Five-Minute Pitch

Here's the pitch you'll make:

> Hi, Mr. Smith, my name is Bill Bartmann. Thank you for taking the time to visit with me. On the phone when we set the appointment I promised that I would only spend five minutes with you.

I'll wait for a response back from you—a smile, frown, grunt, groan, or something. I then say:

> Well I'm really going to keep it exactly to five minutes and that means I have to be efficient about what I have to say. So, Mr. Smith, what I'd really like to do is just lay this all out for you. I've done it in writing and I will give you a copy of it when I leave so you can see exactly what it is I'm offering here. But here's what I'd like to be able to do:
>
> I imagine that you have loans that you no longer are expending your effort and energy trying to collect on. You've already made all the effort you think is worthwhile. You perhaps used your own collection staff or hired one or more outside agencies.

> I would like to make you an offer to purchase those loans from you. If we were able to come to an agreement on that, I think you know whatever amount of money I tender to you would go directly into the profit category, into the capital category of your bank.
>
> Is that something that you have an interest in having a conversation with me about?

If he tells you to continue, then great. This ends the scripted part of the five-minute pitch. But he might go on with some questions:

---

**Mr. Smith:** Why would you want my worst loans?

**You:** Well, Mr. Smith, I'm a student of the industry and I've watched people make millions doing just what I'm proposing. I even know one fellow who made billions of dollars buying bad loans and working out payment plans with those people. He took discounted settlements with the debtors and was able to make a profit because he could spend the time, effort, and energy that most financial institutions really cannot expend on this small portion of their entire book of business.

**Mr. Smith:** What gives you the confidence that your approach will work when not only my crack staff but three other companies I hired—who are absolute professionals at this—were not able to do anything with those loans?

**You:** Well, that is exactly the business risk that I'm prepared to take. I would suggest that if you would allow me the opportunity—and I will sign whatever confidentiality agreement you would have for me—I would do a loan review of the loans you have an interest in selling.

I would be able then to offer you a price for those loans. Quite frankly, I'll only offer you a price that I think I could collect. I'm not saying that someone else did not do a good job; it's just that I

*(continued)*

---

(*continued*)

think I can spend more time on the loans than other people might. As the owner of these loans, I'll be able to work out a payment plan or a settlement over the course of time as these people get back on their feet financially.

**Mr. Smith:** Now, I know you came highly recommended because Mary over at the law firm called me but I gotta understand something. Are you a loan collection company that has long experience in collecting loans?

**You:** No I am not, and I certainly would not want to misrepresent anything to you implicitly or explicitly. Speaking of which, my five minutes is almost up. May I have permission to continue this conversation or would you like me to keep to my five minutes?

**Mr. Smith:** No, that's fine; please continue with your answer to the question. You don't have experience at it, but you're saying that you think you could be more successful than my staff and the collection companies I dealt with?

**You:** First, thank you for allowing me to go beyond that five minutes because this is a great conversation. I'm really hoping we can do some business together that will be fruitful for both your institution and, quite frankly, for myself.

Here is the secret ingredient that I'm able to bring to this program: I know you've collected from most of the people most of the time, and gotten most of the money. I'm willing to bet that there's still some left in there.

Mr. Smith, it's kind of like the mine tailings at a mine. The mining company is only interested in going after the vein of ore and that's where their highest and best use is. It doesn't serve the mining company very well to go out there on the tailings and scrounge through all that stuff.

Well, scavengers can scrounge through that stuff and that's kind of what I am in this business. I know that doesn't have a very nice connotation in some circles but I'm going be able to spend the time on your mine tailings. We both know there is a little bit of gold out there, just not very much.

**Mr. Smith:** Well, I like what I hear so far. But to tell you the truth, Mr. Bartmann, my main concern is, I don't know you from a mashed potato sandwich. I know Mary likes you and that's great. But the only way that I can think of that would allow you to extract more dollars from those mine tailings than I've been able to do is if you use strong-arm collection tactics. That's the last thing this bank needs.

**You:** Mr. Smith, thank you for pointing that out. I think the truth is sometimes counterintuitive.

You know the person I referred to earlier, who became a billionaire in the collection business? I've studied him, and am working with him to learn more. This person did exactly that which I'm proposing to do with you. He became a billionaire not by being a strong-arm collector, but by being a soft-arm collector.

He was actually credited with revolutionizing the collection industry in America by treating customers with dignity and respect. He proved that the concept works 100 times better than strong-arm tactics. I am a disciple of his and a student of his approach.

I think we can collect more than has been collected by working with these people to a degree that your bank might not have been able to. For example, if somebody owes you $1,000 I can't imagine the bank would find it efficient to take payments of $10 a month.

*(You wait for a reaction.)*

Well, I can wait for those payments.

## Analysis of the Meeting

I laid out a very long series of questions, not because I predict that all of them will be asked. They probably won't. I simply want you to hear the whole story, and build your confidence about the themes you're trying to convey.

Consider what you're selling at this moment: You only want permission to review files that are old, dead, and worthless to the bank. You've given a plausible argument about why you may be able to extract value. And when you were asked direct questions about your experience, you said you had none. You then explained that the concepts have been tested and proven, even if you are new to them.

At this point, Frank Smith's unlikely to be shooing you out of his office. Instead, he may ask a few different questions.

---

**Mr. Smith:** Well, what price do you have in mind?

**You:** As much as I'd like to give you a price right now, I'm not able to. I don't know what you have in those files. I don't even know how many there are or specifically what I can collect until I review them.

Again, I have no problem signing a confidentiality agreement. Of course, the better your previous collectors, the less gold is left in those mine tailings. That obviously will affect what I'm able to pay.

But let's look at it from the positive side: Anything I can afford to pay—based on what I think is gold in the tailings—will be profit for you. All I need is permission to do the file review.

**Mr. Smith:** But do you even have a ballpark idea of the kind of money we're talking about?

**You:** Well, again it depends on a number of factors—but how much have you collected off them in the last year?
(*Before he answers, say,*)
I will make this more attractive than that.

---

I still haven't bid, but I've just told him he's going to make more money from me than he made all of last year trying to collect on those assets. I am a profit scenario for him.

**Mr. Smith:** How long do you think it's going to take you?

**You:** That is a function of how many loans you have in your charge-off category, and how accessible the files are—for instance, whether they are paper files, on microfiche, or whatever. Once I've had the opportunity to review a sample of them, I should be able to give you a pretty accurate time estimate.

**Mr. Smith:** Okay, this has been interesting. I have to think about it and I'll get back to you.

**You:** That sounds good, Mr. Smith. I'd like to leave this proposal with you. What would be a reasonable period of time after which I should contact you?

Follow whatever Mr. Smith says in terms of timing, down to the letter. Don't call a day earlier or a day later. Establish your reliability from the get-go.

## Now You're on Your Way

After you leave the meeting with Mr. Smith, your professional business plan will continue to do the talking on your behalf.

Here's what is going through Frank Smith's brain:

- Let's see: I'm making no money on those boxes of dead loan files in my basement.
- This guy wants to pay me some money for them.
- I don't know how much he'll pay, but it's more than I'm making now.
- He *sounds* professional, even though he doesn't have experience in collections.
- All he's asking for right now is the ability to review the basement files.

There's an excellent chance that Frank's going to shrug his shoulders and decide, "What the heck—maybe this guy is for real. I can't see that I have anything to lose by at least playing along and seeing what price he quotes me."

After the meeting, you can make an excellent impression by jotting a quick, *hand-written* note to Mr. Smith:

---

Dear Mr. Smith,

Thanks very much for taking the time today to meet with me. I hope that I answered some of your questions, and that my materials cover the proposal I am making. I stand ready to answer other questions you may have.

I look forward to the possibility of reviewing your non-performing loans and formulating a price that I would be prepared to pay you.

Thanks again for your time.

Sincerely,

Bill Bartmann

---

By the way, in case you would like to see a model confidentiality agreement, you can download one from my web site at www .RoadToMajorWealth.com. Simply go to that site and type into the search box the word "confidential."

## In the Next Chapter

If you follow this approach, you will succeed. Will it happen your first time out? Maybe. Will it happen if you keep at it? Definitely yes.

Should you resist skipping steps and "improving" on my approach? Absolutely.

I think I can speak from experience, given that my company ended up with more than $15 billion of loans in thousands of portfolios. When I was not yet a billionaire, or not even yet a millionaire, I personally visited many banks using the approach I just described, and I was successful. It's a fast road to success, believe me.

In the next chapter, we discuss how to perform a thorough analysis on those loans.

# CHAPTER 6

# How to Review a Loan Portfolio

Congratulations. You've made a lot of progress up to this point. You not only understand the opportunity this business has to offer, but you've taken action. You located a bank and worked your way up the chain to a decision maker. You pitched that person on the possibility of selling you some of the bank's charged-off loans. You asked permission to review those loans, and now you've been ushered into a room with a bunch of file boxes.

I'm not being sarcastic when I say you deserve congratulations. You've come a long way. Now it's time to open those file folders and make sense of what's inside.

I realize that you may not actually be in the basement of a bank, because you might have taken the option to work through a broker, for instance. In that case, the process will be largely the same; you'll simply be doing it electronically.

The loan review is the heart of this entire process. Eventually it's where you want to spend a lot of time getting to be very good. That's because it forms the foundation for the entire deal.

You are formulating a price, and planting a stake in the ground. If you are willing to pay too much, then there goes your investment: You'll need to work extremely hard just to break even, never mind make a profit.

If you bid too little, then you run a risk of the seller saying, "No, thanks." In that case you might have landed the deal, but were not willing to pay a realistic price.

Warning: Don't take a "yes" or "no" from the seller as an indication that you paid too little or too much. You could get a "no" even if your offer was extremely generous. On other occasions, you may get a "yes" even though you offered absurdly little money for some reason. Especially when you're dealing with local banks, this will be a loose, inefficiently priced market.

There is a permanent display in the Smithsonian Institution recognizing the groundbreaking work my company did in this area. I won't bore you with the details, except to say that we used human systems and computer systems to turn the loan review process into a science. Our research was so vast that I was told the only entity on earth with more data than we had was the National Security Agency.

I'm telling you that as a way of emphasizing how incredibly valuable this process can be to your business. There is no limit to how rich you can become if you get really good at this. Fortunately, you can get started—and make surprisingly good judgments—by just applying common sense and a methodical attitude.

## Factors That Affect Loan Collectability

At my company we refined and developed 64 separate factors that went into our analysis of each loan. That's well beyond what you need to do with that First National Bank box. It is, however, something for you to shoot for over time.

Let's look at the main categories of factors.

## Area-Related Factors

### State Laws Relating to Statutes of Limitations
We covered this before. You should know how much time is left on the loans, in terms of when they will become uncollectible because they're past the statute of limitations.

### Communities Where the Borrowers Are Located
Use your knowledge of communities to gauge whether they're generally on the upswing, downswing, or fairly steady. That does not necessarily relate to a given loan. However, if it's been common knowledge that a region has been hard-hit for decades, you should note that in the file.

### Major Employers Moving in and out of the Area
If a U.S. automaker pulled out of a town in Ohio, that's pretty significant bad news for thousands of previously solid borrowers in that area. Conversely, a Japanese automaker announcing a new plant in Georgia might mean that borrowers in that area will soon be back to work.

### Work Ethic
I know it's hard to pin down statistically, but you may be able to make distinctions based on your knowledge of the presence or absence of a work ethic in the community.

## Enforceability Factors

### Signatures
You will see a copy of the *note* or contract. Does it have signatures in all the blanks, or are some missing? It happens. If that's the case, you will have more difficulty enforcing the unsigned contract.

### Capacity

This refers to *mental capacity*, or ability of the borrower even to sign a document and have it be legally binding. Contracts with minors would be a problem. You may see mention of competency hearings, *special powers of attorney*, and so on.

### Death

Is there any indication that the person is dead? If so, is the estate still open and could it be pursued? This should generate a scribbled note by you to check on that.

### Bankruptcy

This would most likely put an end to collection efforts. Is there any note to the effect that a bankruptcy occurred or is being contemplated?

### Improper Underwriting

Does the file contain any documents regarding claims by the borrower that the contract is not legally enforceable or that the lender took some action that is improper?

## Ability and Inclination of Borrowers to Pay

After you establish that the contract appears to be legally enforceable, then focus on the borrower's inclination and ability to repay.

A file full of collection actions—with no success—may make it seem like the borrower is never to be trusted. However, keep in mind that at some point in the past, this person was considered a bank-quality borrower, or would not have gotten the loan.

### Payment History

You should see detailed notes about which payments were made and when they became less regular and eventually stopped.

### Offers to Settle

Look for copies of correspondence sent to or from the borrower. Do you see any attempt by the borrower to reach a settlement or establish a repayment plan? These are good signs.

### Inability versus Unwillingness to Pay

Some borrowers are beset by major medical bills or some other catastrophe. They would like nothing more than to pay their debts, and in fact they previously did so. These might be situations where—when their circumstances improve—they'll be ready to make payments again.

### Effort by Lender to Resolve the Debt

Is there evidence of a significant volume of correspondence between the lender and borrower? This is often the result of a disagreement about repayment terms or other issues. Over time, I found that this is a pretty good indicator of the unwillingness of a borrower to repay, as counterintuitive as that may seem.

### Credit Bureau Report

Is there a recent one in the file? If so, really study it. The report will tell you how the borrower is handling other obligations. It will also give you clues about address, employer, length of employment, marital status, and so on. There may be evidence of untapped lines of credit, or other banking relationships. These are good signs.

Before you own the portfolio of loans, you will have no legal right to pull a credit report. However, you should ask the bank if it could pull the reports as part of your review.

If they say "okay," then great. You now will have detailed and fresh information. If they say, "Heck no, that will cost us money!" then you just made it easier to negotiate a lower price for the portfolio. You can later justifiably claim, "If I had fresh information while formulating my offer, the numbers could well be higher."

By the way, once you own the loan, you should almost always pull a credit report. It has too much good information to be ignored, even though it will cost you money to pull it. The exceptions would be a tiny loan or really bad circumstances indicated in the file.

### Home Ownership
The credit report may indicate if the borrower owns a home. You should also see years at current and prior residences. If it's been long-term home ownership, this could indicate a borrower with a willingness to pay in the right circumstances.

### Financial Statements
Even if these are outdated, they can reveal assets that could be converted to cash. They may also disclose a profession, skill or trade, or other indications of stability.

### Tax Returns
These are also sources of a wealth of information, similar to credit reports. You can discover address, spousal information, wages, investments, social security number, and a variety of assets and business ventures.

### Employment
Indications of long-term employment in the past are a positive sign. The same is true of skilled craftspeople or professionals. It's no guarantee of anything, but again may point toward a willingness to settle debts.

### Loan Application
This may reveal other facts not found on the documents above.

### Additional Guarantors
Did anyone co-sign or guarantee the debt? What notes indicate that these people have been contacted to make good on the guarantee?

### Age and Health
Very old people may be less likely to repay, as would people with serious illnesses.

## Collateral Factors

### Lien Perfection
This refers to whether the debt obligation was ever recorded at the registry of deeds or other legal repository of records. This is often helpful in enforcing obligations, because a lien can prevent a borrower from taking out a new loan before settling old debts.

### Lien Priority
Where are you in the pecking order of debts to be repaid?

### Recoverability
Is the item that was pledged as collateral easily recovered in the event of repossession? Small items are easy to hide.

### Liquidity
Is there an established market for the collateral?

## Special Considerations

### Lack of Documentation
Is there insufficient information in the file in order to formulate an opinion of value?

### Litigious Borrower
Does the file contain information that indicates a borrower who's either considering litigation, or has gone ahead with it? This could indicate problems with the original loan, or counter-claims the borrower could make.

### Language Barriers
Does the file indicate that the borrower can understand and speak English? Does it indicate that the borrower has access to someone who can act as interpreter? This may be a positive, in the event that you could find someone to communicate with the borrower.

## How to Put It All Together

I hope you're beginning to appreciate the wealth of information you can discover in the loan file. You must approach this research with the spirit of Sherlock Holmes, from the famous British detective stories. He would solve great mysteries by observing seemingly minor clues and knitting them together to explain what happened.

You can do the same. The bank and previous collection agencies may have been very thorough—or they may have breezed over certain factors that jump out at you. I can assure you that some agencies are much more thorough than others.

### Scoring

All of the factors I just laid out for you are considerations, but they take a human to evaluate them. I never reduced them to a simple score. For instance, I did not think that if a language barrier is an issue, that's a reduction in the score by 0.5 percent, or if the borrower is a medical doctor the score increases by 1.3 percent.

I wouldn't trust such results. Instead, I created a system where highly experienced people could scan a loan file and quickly recognize the problems and possibilities.

You can do the same when you're armed with my list and the attitude of Sherlock Holmes. Will it take you longer than it took one of my expert analysts? Of course. So what. You're not trying to break a speed record; you're trying to make money. It's potentially a highly profitable use of your time.

Therefore, review the file and make your own separate notes in your own notepad. Keep referring to my list of factors. While reviewing a loan file, you may see a deal killer: For instance, if the borrower filed bankruptcy, assign that file a score of zero.

On the other hand, you may see that the borrower stopped paying when a business partnership was breaking up two years ago. That problem may be resolved by now, and the borrower may be willing to restart payments.

## It's All about ECR

That stands for Estimated Cash Recovery, and it's the single most important measure in assessing a loan.

ECR is the percentage of the loan's *face value* that you expect you can recover. It forms the basis for what you will offer to the bank for the loans in the first place. It also will be your guide over time to how you're doing in the collection process.

We generally used 24 months as the period for estimating collections. We might try to collect on loans beyond 24 months, assuming we thought there was value and the statute of limitations had not run out. But it's a good benchmark for estimating the total potential collectability of loans.

Try to approach every asset with the assumption that it has zero value to start with. Your mission is to identify those factors indicating that the asset does have value. For instance, you might notice that the borrower was good at payments until a certain date when a sudden drop-off occurred. It might not be explained in the notes. That could indicate someone with the willingness to pay, but with circumstances that—if they ever go away—might once again pay.

Remember that with the first portfolio of loans I did, I walked into the file room with no clue about what I was doing. I did not have the detailed list I just handed you. I had common sense, a pencil, and paper. I assigned my own ECR on the spot.

Here's a tip: Don't sweat the percentages. As consumers, we spend dollars, not percentages, and that's where our best judgment resides. Therefore, after reviewing a loan file, sit back and ask yourself "How many dollars do I think I may be able to get from this borrower?" Then put down a dollar amount in your notes.

Be conservative. The only fatal mistake is bidding too much. You need an overabundance of caution in this business. It's much better to lose the bid than to bid too high.

## Do the Full Review

Do not take merely a sample of the loan file! You must attach a dollar-amount score to each loan. Then it's a matter of adding up the dollar amounts to arrive at what you conservatively think you can collect from that portfolio.

## In the Next Chapter

Even after one session of reviewing loan files, you will not be the same person again. You'll be decoding these files, looking for clues, and seeing more and more dimensions. Will you be unsure of yourself? It's likely. Just remember that you're something of an authority on being a consumer yourself—you've been one for many years. You are now reviewing loan documents of other consumers who have been in familiar situations: just married, lost a job, temporary illness, whatever.

Very quickly you will be able to know if your judgment is off: You'll begin to collect on those loans, and your *estimated* cash recovery will become an *actual* one. Imagine how good you'll become over time!

Before we start the collection process, though, there's the matter of getting the bank to say "yes" to our offer, and to finance that offer if possible. That's what I discuss next.

# 7

# How to Make a Portfolio Offer and Finance It

You had your initial meeting with Frank Smith, president of First National Bank. He was intrigued about your reviewing some of the loans in his boneyard. He granted you access for the file review.

It's possible that Mr. Smith will ask you in advance what you had in mind to pay him. I've already told you to resist that discussion, but I want to emphasize the point. Until the file review is complete, pricing simply cannot be determined.

Let's say you made the mistake of blurting out, "Hey, let me look at your bad loans and I'll give you a nickel on the dollar for them." Now you have a nickel-on-the-dollar hurdle to get over, when just a moment ago the banker had no number at all in his mind. What if you go downstairs and find out they're only collectible at seven or eight cents?

You've just busted the model I will share with you in a moment. Sadly, you will probably consummate and then you're going to wonder why you did a lot of work for not much money. You must instead communicate, "I don't know what it is I will be able to offer you, but let me go look."

The dynamics of this relationship have dramatically shifted, now that you're reviewing the loans. You are not a pest to be batted away by Frank's secretary. You're a brand-new potential profit center for the bank.

He's waiting for you to tell him what the review showed. In fact, he's hoping you'll hurry up and get that review over with. Therefore, once you have permission to review the files, get going. Don't get this far only to say, "Great, Mr. Smith, I'll get right to the review of your files after I come back from my family reunion. It's a weeklong affair we have on Cape Cod every year at this time. . . ."

He had been hoping you would go downstairs today or tomorrow, then come back up and bid crazy. Now, three minutes into your relationship, you've already disappointed him. Strike while Frank Smith is hot.

After the file review, walk upstairs and go to Frank's secretary. As you're dusting the cobwebs off your sleeves, say: "Okay, I'm finished with the review and will now go back to my office to formulate my offer. Would you please schedule an appointment for me to see Mr. Smith?"

I wouldn't be surprised if Frank's door opens about then, because she's got you on speakerphone. Resist the temptation to talk about your findings just yet. You need time to prepare your bid in writing.

## How to Calculate the Bid

In the analysis phase next to each loan, you wrote down a dollar amount you thought you could collect. It might be zero in some cases, and a decent number in others. Then you added up all those numbers and compared the total to the face value of all the loans in the portfolio.

Now calculate the percentage that represents. As I mentioned before, that's your estimated cash recovery (ECR). Let's assume that you think those loans are collectable at 9 percent. I'm just picking a number that's easily divisible. Your mileage may vary.

It's time to give you the Bartmann Formula: *Do not bid more than one-third of your ECR.*

You should have been conservative while going through each file and estimating what you could get from that borrower. In this business, smart people are conservative. In other words, cut that ECR down to one-third and consider that to be your *maximum bid.*

Negotiating tip: *Do not offer your maximum bid right from the outset!* You are setting yourself up for disappointment if you do.

Here's why. You may think that offering what you can offer is just being straightforward. But in the world of negotiating, it's likely that the other person will consider you not only inflexible, but also not to be negotiating in good faith.

If you state your maximum offer, then by definition you cannot move closer to the other person's price. If you do, you've just blown your maximum offer discipline and hurt yourself. If you stick to your guns, then what you're saying is, "My price is my price. End of discussion. If you want to do this deal, you'll have to be the one to demonstrate all the flexibility, because I'm not gonna budge."

You may not mean to come across that way, but your actions will. You're also not doing your negotiating partner any favors. Consider how it will look when Mr. Smith reports back to his bank board. He'll be asked what price he got. Then he may be asked what price he offered and what amount you offered. Now Mr. Smith looks like a weakling to the board members:

> Frank, let me get this straight. This Bartfield guy offered you 3 percent, and you wanted 5. So he stuck to his guns at 3 percent, and you came down to 4. Then he shook his head and stayed at 3 percent, and you caved in at 3? Hey, great going there, Frank!

That's the kind of tough-minded president we need running First National Bank!

If your maximum bid is 3 percent, think about starting out at 2 percent. Then if you need to, work up in fractions, but do not exceed 3 percent.

Once you've made this calculation, convert the initial bid number back to a dollar amount. You'll need that number in a moment.

## How to Prepare the Bid Document

I gotta be honest with you: You do not *need* to prepare a written bid in order to succeed. If you have an overabundance of confidence and a good memory for just what to say, it's possible to go in with no documents. However, I would recommend that you prepare a written bid.

Remember that you have some credibility with the bank, or you wouldn't have gotten this far. Let's not kid ourselves—it's only a small amount of credibility, though. You've sold the banker on a zero-cost proposition of looking at his files and making an offer for assets he considers worthless. You have yet to deliver anything.

Therefore, keep building that credibility up as much as you can. After you do your first deal, the banker will be coming to you and saying, "Hey, want some more loans?"

There's another good reason for preparing a written bid: The decision to sell loans to you will probably be made by more than one person, even if you're negotiating with the president. This is new territory for the bank, after all. You want to put your best foot forward with all those decision makers, in the form of your written bid.

Remember the old "telephone game" where one person whispers to another, who whispers to another? By about the fourth person, the message is unrecognizable from what the first person told the second. You do not want that happening with your bid!

## What's on the Bid

This is not a complicated document. The banker really only cares about one thing, which starts with a dollar sign.

Here is what you *do not* want to do under any circumstances: Do not show the banker your loan-by-loan analysis. I know: You think it will be impressive. It will backfire on you, though.

When you're down to dollars in a negotiation, you must adhere to the KISS Principle: Keep It Simple, Stupid. If you get mired in looking at dozens of loans, one or more of four things will happen:

1. You'll bore the banker, who now has lost interest and may be late for his next appointment.
2. He'll start to argue with you about this loan versus that loan.
3. You've now shown him all your cards, and that's no way to play poker.
4. He will make a mental note of the loans you marked with the highest potential collectability, and send them out for collection himself, cutting you out of the best loans in the box. How do I know this? It happened to me.

I am not suggesting that you deceive the banker. I am suggesting that you simply keep some negotiating room for yourself.

Your bid should show a breakdown of what you found, as shown in Table 7.1. You want to reinforce the fact that you methodically

**Table 7.1** Results of Your Search

| Category | Percentage of Total Loans |
| --- | --- |
| Deceased | 11 |
| Bankrupt | 14 |
| Skipped/Unknown Address | 22 |
| No contact for five or more years | 36 |
| Other | 17 |

went through all those loan documents with a professional approach. You will accomplish that if the banker sees results as explained in Table 7.1.

You will know all these numbers from your research. You're now stating what the banker kind of already knew, but you will now confirm: It's not a pretty box of loans.

You need not interpret those numbers for the banker on paper. They speak for themselves.

Below these results you have the amount of what you are prepared to bid. This is important: *Do it as a dollar amount—not a percentage*.

None of us are paid in percentages. We carry dollars in our pocket. If you want to get a visceral, positive reaction, talk about the dollars you are about to give the banker.

That's all the document contains. Don't hand it over just yet, though, because I need to explain something.

## How You Conduct the Meeting

Remember when you first met with Mr. Smith? You should have had a confident and hopeful tone to your voice, telegraphing that you have some good news: You want to hand him money for assets in his basement—assets he thinks are worthless.

That is not the tone you will now telegraph. When you walk in, be polite and don't overdo it, but have a somewhat disappointed look on your face.

> Hello, Mr. Smith. Thanks for taking the time to meet with me to go over what I found after reviewing your loan files. Honestly, I'm a bit disappointed. You've done a great job! Your loan collectors have really done better than what I've heard is the industry standard for loans at this phase. Your staff is to be complimented.

*(Later, when you have a track record, you can replace that sentence with "Your loan collectors have really done better than what I've seen in other financial institutions.")*

Here's what just happened: Mr. Smith was hopeful—or at least intrigued—with the prospect of your bounding up the stairs and offering him a pile of dough. You did not do that. Still, it takes him only a moment to process your words and realize that he's in agreement. He thought all along that those loans were lost causes. That's why they're in the boneyard.

A moment later, Mr. Smith feels good again. He realizes that he can tell the bank board that an independent third party has just validated that the First National Bank staff did a good job with loan collections. He wants to believe that, and you just said it was true.

You have now set the expectation that there is very little value in that box of loans. At this point, Mr. Smith should be figuring that you just might thank him for his time and say that you uncovered nothing of value, but you appreciate having the opportunity to try. Now you continue:

I went through that entire box, loan by loan. I actually reviewed each loan with 29 factors in mind. *(Those are the 29 loan review elements in the previous chapter.)*

I won't bore you with the excruciating details, because I know you realize that each delinquent borrower has a long story of why he or she can't pay. But you may be interested in a few statistics I gathered.

*(This is where you read from your written bid, but do not yet hand it to Mr. Smith. If you do, he just stopped paying attention to you and is only focused on the paper.)*

I found that 11 percent of the borrowers are deceased, 14 percent declared bankruptcy, 22 percent of borrowers appear to have skipped town or at least their current address is unknown, and fully 36 percent of the portfolio are people with whom there's been no collection contact for five or more years.

*(continued)*

(*continued*)

(*Pause to let that sink in.*)

Still, you've been kind enough to let me review these files in detail. I am willing to see if I can extract some little value from this loan portfolio, even though all previous efforts were unsuccessful. Here's what I'm able to pay you for these charged-off loans.

Now you hand Mr. Smith the printed bid and—this is very important—*you shut up and sit there.*

You do know the most fundamental rule in closing a sale, don't you? After the offer is made, the person who speaks next is the one in the weaker position. Let Mr. Smith be on the hot seat now.

He's staring at a dollar figure that may be less than he fantasized over the last couple of days. Still, he says to himself, it is money that his bank had never expected. It's *found money*. It's compelling, as long as you don't blow it by chattering at this stage.

Naturally, you're home free if he hems and haws and finally says, "Well, I guess something's better than nothing. I was planning on burning 'em anyway, so it looks like you have a deal."

On the other hand, he may want to see how much he can get, if only to answer the board member who later will ask, "Did you push him, Frank? Did you negotiate hard?"

So Frank may look disappointed himself right about now. He's in a quandary, because he wants to believe that he's already extracted all the money that was in that loan portfolio. But he does not want to cave in without any resistance. Finally he figures out what to say.

Well, Mr. Bartmann, I can see your point. And I do know that my bank is regarded as having one of the most effective and professional collection departments in the area. Still, I was hoping you were going to bid a lot more than that, because it isn't worth our time and trouble to do the paperwork for that amount. Well, heck, that's only—what is that? Whoa, that's only 2 percent.

Now it's his turn to go silent. You think about it and say:

> Mr. Smith, I know 2 percent sounds like a small number, but 2 percent against the million dollars in face value of loans that are sitting downstairs? That's $20,000 that goes on your books tomorrow. And it's for files you were going to burn.

It's like the reverse of Las Vegas where you play with chips. In Vegas, they will not allow money on the table. They learned long ago that people will spend more in pretty plastic chips than if money is staring them in the face.

In our case, we want to drive home the point that you are offering honest-to-goodness American greenbacks for worthless boxes of files, so we talk up the dollar amount.

If he now agrees, then great. If he still is having a hard time, this is the time to appear that you are the one caving in and speaking first, because you say:

> The only way I could ever do any more than that is if you carried the paper. If you were able to finance it, I could probably go up to $30,000.

Frank now is feeling better, and this is the logic that's going through his head:

> *Hmmm, that's 3 percent. That's better than nothing. If I put $30,000 on the books and this guy only pays me half of it before he goes broke—Okay . . . I've then got 15,000 bucks more than I had before. It's also $15,000 more than we made last year on those crappy loans.*

Wait and see what he comes back with.

> But, Bill, how can I honestly say to the guy that the most I can pay him is 2 percent, and then tell him a few minutes later that I can now pay him three percent?

It isn't what I can collect. It's what it's going to cost me to get the financing, plus the time, effort, and energy it would take to go to another institution. I'll need to write up a loan proposal for them and go through a whole process.

> Bill, will he think I'm small potatoes because I don't whip out my checkbook and pay him cash?

First, he knows you are not Big Potatoes, or you wouldn't be down in his basement, going through charged-off loan files. But if it makes you feel any better, my company owned $15 *billion* in loans from 800 different financial institutions, and they were all 100 percent financed. In fact, I've never put down a penny of my own money to finance any of the 4.5 million loans I've been involved with—ever.

> What if he instead says, "I understand if I would carry the paper you would pay me $30,000. But I cannot finance it, so will you pay me two percent in cash after all?"

That's when I would say:

I can understand that you cannot finance it. I'm going to need a little time to get my financing in place. If you're not able to carry it at $30,000, let me see if I can find the $20,000 somewhere else. I did not put the financing in place because I just assumed and believed that you would have an interest in doing this transaction.

At this point if he says, "No, I really can't lend you the money," I would be a little disappointed, but not a lot. Why?

Because he's just implied that he'll do the transaction at 2 percent. He didn't come out and say that, but look at what else he did not say. He didn't say "I can't believe you offered me only 2 percent for these loans!" How could he claim that if he thought all along that the loans were worthless. No, I'm pretty sure that I've got a deal at least at 2 percent, because he wasn't resisting me there. I just need to get the financing for two percent.

By the way, does he really want to send me across the street? With my financing comment about paying him 3 percent, I've just given him a reason to finance me. If I go across the street and that banker says, "You mean you buy bad loans and you're going to buy the First National bad loans and you're going to pay Smith $20,000? We've got some loans downstairs. You want to see ours?"

So I'm not feeling bad because I now have a file review done. Remember that I'm confident that I can collect 9 percent on this portfolio. I now know I can buy it for 2 percent from Mr. Smith.

If I have to, I go down the street to the other bank. This is no longer a two-party transaction, but a three-party one: First National Bank, me, and the other bank that will finance the loans. I explain three-party transactions a bit later.

Bill, what if a banker asks to see my detailed research on each loan, to support the number I'm offering him?

You must be very cautious about this, and that's why I suggest you not have it with you when you meet.

If you show them your set of numbers—which I strongly urge you not to—you'd better have a reason why you need the margin that you're asking for. If my detailed analysis indicates I think I can collect 9 percent and I'm only bidding two, that raises a question.

I would need to say:

> I know this financing process to pay you the 2 percent will take time, effort, and energy on my part. So that's really like $2^1/_2$ to 3 percent by the time I'm done, depending on what I end up going through.
>
> Then I need a three-to-one relationship between collectability and my bid, or this just doesn't make good sense to me. That's the formula that my mentor, Bill Bartmann, espouses. This guy literally became a billionaire buying these kinds of loans, so I'm deferring to him and this formula is what it's going to take. So 3 percent is my high number and that's only if I get financing.

You could say all that, but I would not do so unless I was really pressed on the issue, and I thought it spelled the difference between losing a great deal and getting it.

> Bill, would you ever suggest that I maintain two different spreadsheets of my analysis—the real one, and then the one I would show a bank with the lower number?

Never. Either don't show the banker or show him the truth. Do not play games with the truth. It's bad business to have two sets of books—to tell a lie and then try to support it with paperwork.

You should instead say, "I'm sorry, but that's confidential," or, "That's private information," or simply "I'm really not prepared to show that."

If it means that the transaction doesn't happen, then it doesn't happen. Your integrity is intact, which is much more important than any one transaction.


## The Conclusion of the Meeting

I have given you no theory here. I've laid out the way to conduct the meeting, because I've done it successfully many times myself using just this approach.

Remember that there are plenty of fish in this ocean. You're not begging for business; in fact, you are doing the bank a service by paying good money for bad loans—even if that money is financed by the bank itself.


## Get the Deal in Writing

When you land your first deal—and every one after that—you must use a document to cement the handshake.

I strongly recommend that you not leave it up to the bank to come up with the agreement. If you do, you'll have the bank's attorney hand you something that includes the kitchen sink, because it's an unusual sale. Attorneys get nervous about unusual sales, and they tend to go overboard on the contract language. On my web site at www.RoadToMajorWealth.com, I have a sample Loan Sale Agreement. You can get it by typing the word "loan" into the search box.

You still must run it by your own attorney, because I am not representing that it will work for all loan types in all states. Still, it will get you headed in the right direction.

If you are buying loan portfolios from the government or from brokers, you'll be using their documents.

## Financing Your Portfolio

You'll be surprised at how many banks will not only have charged-off loans for you to purchase, but will finance 100 percent of your purchase. They'll use the bad loans you buy as collateral for the loan.

I suggest that when you are starting out in this business, try to do a deal with a local bank that will finance its own paper. Then do the same with every other bank within your comfortable driving range. Only after you've exhausted those bank opportunities in your area do you need to step up to three-way transactions.

Can you do a three-way one right from the start? Sure. But keep in mind that the two-party transactions are the easiest of all. There is no need to explain the nature of the portfolio, because the bank knows its own loans. The two-party lender really is not concerned about a lot of detail.

It's *found money*. In effect, you're giving a great deal to the bank. You do not say the following, but it's what they hear:

> I would like to work my butt off to try to collect on your loans. You've been unsuccessful at it, but I'd like to try a different approach. And by the way, you get to keep the first $30,000 of what I recover, and I get to keep whatever I recover beyond that.

> Bill, let's say I get the financing directly from the bank. I get the package and I feel like, hey, this is all coming together. Then something happens and I'm not able to work that loan package and at least get the financing back, never mind my profit. What happens to me?

It depends. If you signed something that gave the bank your personal guarantee for that borrowing, you would have the same repercussions as if you bought an automobile that you then sold and it had a deficiency balance. You become liable. It's whatever the terms of the loan agreement that you negotiate state.

The banker will of course prefer for you to have personal liability. That's why I recommend that you be conservative not only when looking at each loan, but you then bid no more than one-third of what you conservatively think you can collect. Are you taking a wild risk? No. Are you taking a calculated risk? Yes.

If you think you can't collect even one-third of your conservative loan analysis, then you should not engage. On the other hand, if you think you can collect it, welcome to the American capitalist system where we get to gamble that we're going to be right. If we win, we win. If we lose, we lose. That's no different from any other business transaction in the entire world.

## You're Not in a Financial Catch-22 in This Business

If you have any experience with real estate investing, you know the problem I'm describing: Let's say you're starting out as an investor, and you locate a nice property. You want to buy it in order to resell it to someone else.

Before you can get serious with many sellers, you must show *proof of funds*. They do not want to take their property off the market only to waste time on somebody who can't get financing.

The problem for a new investor is that in order to show proof of funds you must go to a lender. That lender wants to see the details of the investment, but you don't have the deal yet—you're in a circular situation because you cannot satisfy either party.

The beauty of the loan business is that as a brand-new participant, you don't have the same catch-22 to contend with:

- When you're buying the First National Bank's charged-off loans, it knows full well what those loans are about. Frank

Smith has the power to let you look at them for as long as you wish.

- When you buy from a loan broker, the same is true: The broker will encourage you to perform due diligence on the loan portfolio before bidding. It won't cost you a penny. Later he'll want to know you're good for any money you bid on the portfolio, but not now.

- Even when you're buying from the FDIC, you don't need to put any money down in order to review the loans. The time for a deposit is when you want to place a bid.

With this flexibility, you can really study the portfolio in order to get comfortable with its potential value. Furthermore, you'll have lots of detail on which to base your overall bid price.

## How to Get 100 Percent Financing to Acquire Loans

I've already described how to go about getting your portfolio financed by the very bank whose portfolio you're buying. That's called a *two-party transaction*. Such seller financing will only happen at a bank. You will not get it from a loan broker or from the government.

We're now going to see how to negotiate a three-party transaction, where you buy the portfolio from one bank but have it financed by another financial institution.

Before I do that, I can see an objection that might get in the way of your giving me your full attention.

> But, Bill, when you started your company, the banking environment was different. Now, you just have to read the newspapers to see that banks are not even lending to each other. You still think I can walk down the street and get a bank loan for someone else's portfolio?

Yes, I do.

First, understand that when I started in this business, we were in the middle of a recession. The Good Times were nowhere in sight. In fact, around 2,500 banks had failed or were in the process of doing so around the time I started out. The techniques I describe worked then, and will work in the current recession, too.

Second, there's an aspect of the banking business that never makes it to the newspapers or television broadcasts. Because my company had developed relationships with 21 of the top 25 banks in America—and over 800 financial institutions in total—I know a thing or two about how lenders work.

It's true that in late 2008, the credit markets froze up. I need to describe what I mean by *credit markets*: Major banks would not lend to other major banks for esoteric instruments like securitizations, derivatives, senior subordinated debt, and so on. We've all heard the stories of Wall Street firms getting into trouble by creating exotic products like *credit default swaps*. Many of these products blew up in the faces of bankers who pretended they knew what kind of devices they were playing with. They didn't.

Many of the large transactions for such instruments ground to a halt in 2008. Then something else happened. Even though your local banks were not engaging in these types of transactions at all, they were spooked.

It's kind of like being on the beach when somebody sees a shark. There's only one shark and it probably will affect only the people currently out there in the water. Still, people on the shore are scared to death and they swear they'll not go back in the water ever. The banking system overreacted.

Let's now look at that local bank more closely. The bank's source of revenue—and of existence—consists of taking in deposits at a given interest rate, and lending money at a higher rate. Its profit is the difference between what it pays depositors and what it's paid by borrowers.

The bank can quit lending in the same fashion as you can decide to jump in a pool, sink to the bottom, and hold your breath.

That is exactly what's going on. Banks are holding their breath, but they can't hold their breath long or they turn blue. In fact, this is what very smart people like Treasury Secretary Henry Paulson saw in 2008. Even the big banks with the most assets were holding their breath.

Because Paulson was previously chairman of Goldman Sachs, he was extremely familiar with the signals banks were giving. The Big Boys were turning blue. That's why he made it clear that the banking system was on the verge of keeling over. The $700 billion rescue plan was an emergency room resuscitation to get those banks' hearts—their lending—going again.

It's no different on Main Street. They didn't seize up quite as badly because they were not lending on funky esoteric investments. Still, they simply cannot hold their breath for long.

Besides, when you walk in the door, you're asking for a loan on a good old American asset they've dealt with for years and know all about: their bad loans.

Again, don't try to go into a local branch of a giant national bank chain and ask for financing on a bad-loan portfolio. Their strict rules from headquarters allow them zero room to be creative with you. Now, if you simply want to go in there and make the financing presentation as a way of honing your skills, more power to you.

## How to Find the Bank That Will Finance You

You're probably ahead of me at this point: You're guessing that I'll say: "Start with the bank where you have a relationship," and you're right.

If you've been banking somewhere already, you have several built-in brownie points. They've been earning money on your account and credit card fees; you might also have one or more loans through them; and they may have pulled your credit report and offered you still other services like home equity loans. You're one of the Good Guys in the eyes of your bank.

Those factors aren't so compelling that the banker will say, "I'll make you a loan because you bank with us." But compared to another person who's not a customer but also wants a loan, the bank likes you a little better.

If you do not have any relationships with banks, then you can always just call them up and arrange for an appointment with someone in the lending department. You're not intruding, you understand: The lending department needs to be busy lending money or those nice people will soon get a pink-colored envelope.

Be prepared to go to several banks before you find one that finances your portfolio. Think how good you'll get at honing your presentation after each meeting. Not only will you eventually be successful, but that bank will be more than happy to finance further portfolios for its newest profitable customer—you.

## Essential Ingredients for Securing Your Loan

### Business Plan

You brought a business plan into Frank Smith at First National Bank in order to convince him to allow you to review his charged-off loans. That's the same business plan you will use now to convince your lender that you're a professional. You will reference the business plan in your loan proposal. More on that in a minute.

### Portfolio Review

Here you detail the score you assigned to every single loan and the reasons for assigning that particular score to that loan. It documents that there is sufficient collectability from the loans within the portfolio in order for the lender to be repaid.

In case you think I'm flip-flopping from what I said in an earlier chapter, I'm not: With the two-party approach, I want

Frank Smith to finance my purchase of his own loans. Mr. Smith already knows the loans in his basement. When you ask him for a loan, again he's making a calculation: "Let's see, this Bartmann guy may actually be able to extract some value from the loans, in which case we get the first money, until he pays us back. Any money he pays us is more than we're getting today on those loans."

When you go into a third-party bank to get financing to buy somebody else's loans you want to walk in with all of the spreadsheets you can muster. You want to overwhelm the lender with how thorough you've been. It supports the conclusion that you're an acceptable risk to lend money to.

Here's another difference: In the two-party transaction, no one else needs to know what you think is collectible on those loans. Either your price is acceptable, or it's not.

When it's a three-party transaction, you need to tell the banker what you think is collectible, loan by loan. Show him each individual review. Lay all your spreadsheets out on the table. He may not even pay much attention to them once he realizes that you paid attention. But it supports your request for the loan and that you've done your homework on this business opportunity. You cannot be too specific here.

In fact, you should ask if there's someone at the bank with whom you could sit down to review your analysis in detail. It's a nice touch.

Give them every opportunity to concur with your conclusions. Occasionally you will have someone quibble with your estimate of a loan's collectability: You're too high; you're too low. That's fine. Remember, nobody knows the real answer. The only proof comes when you call this guy and try to collect. Until then it's just supposition and opinion.

If the third-party bank gets that involved in reviewing your loan portfolio, it's a very good sign. It's impressed with your work, and is interested in confirming the details, or it wouldn't be going to the bother of discussing individual loans. You're almost there.

## Loan Proposal

The document that is likely to put your loan request over the top and get it funded is the loan proposal.

When 99.9 percent of people need a loan, they go about it the wrong way:

95 *percent* of them walk into the bank and the extent of their preparation is to say, "I need me a new holding tank for my landscaping business and I need to borrow $95,000. Will you lend it to me?"

4.9 *percent* of the remaining people come in with shoeboxes of documents and reams of files. They're trying to look impressive, but the loan officer is groaning under the prospect that he'll have to wade through all that stuff.

0.1 *percent* of people have a well-constructed loan proposal that lays out exactly what the bank cares about. It telegraphs that you are a professional who respects the bank's time and need for specific information.

# Loan Proposal Principles

### Always Deliver Your Proposal in Writing

Any organization of decent size has a hierarchy of employees. Because lending decisions are so important to a bank, they're done by some of the more senior people.

Those are not likely to be the people you meet when you first apply for the loan. Therefore, your challenge is to get your message through to all the parties involved. It must be a clear message, and not muddied by the faulty memory of a front-line person you talked to.

When you create a thorough and professional loan proposal, it will continue to impress readers long after you drive out of the bank parking lot. When done right, it will do the selling for you.

## The Person Taking Your Application Cannot Say Yes, but Can Say No

Front-line employees are paid to screen out all the tire-kickers and casual visitors, and only let the serious customers through to more senior bank staff.

You may have a most spectacular loan portfolio that needs financing, but if you're not professionally persistent, you can easily get derailed. The front-line person could say, "We don't make loans like that." That may even be true—up until now. You must remain polite and not talk down to this person, who's in a position to file your proposal in the round container next to her feet.

Instead it's better to start by calling the switchboard and asking for the name of the person in charge of making business loans. Similar to the process we covered for getting to Mr. Smith at First National Bank, you can call this loan officer and ask for five minutes of her time. In this case, you'll be welcomed even more readily because it sounds like you want to become a new borrower for the bank. Then when you visit the bank, you'll be walking in with an appointment to see a senior person.

## Contents of the Loan Proposal

Remember what I said earlier: Most people either walk in unprepared and ask for a loan, or they shovel a ton of semi-relevant paper at someone.

The way you will stand out like a diamond is to make your loan proposal as thin as possible, while still answering all the questions the loan officer will have. You're shooting for "comprehensive but quick." That's exactly what I've laid out for you here:

### Executive Summary Sheet

This is a summary of the type of loan you're asking for. Simply take two or three paragraphs to explain your project as clearly and succinctly as you can.

You might write this page last, after you've assembled the other sections. It will make it easier to summarize when everything is fresh in your mind.

### Term Sheet

This is one page, with the skeletal outlines of the loan laid out in bullet points. My comments are in parentheses:

- **Amount**—(The amount of money you're asking for.)
- **Type of Loan**—(You would say something like "Amortized over 36 months" or "No interest for 12 months and balloon at 5 years." There is no one right term. It's all negotiable.)
- **Interest Rate**—(If you don't know what the going rate is for such loans, a ballpark is prime plus 2 percent. It's just a starting place.)
- **Method of Repayment**—("Monthly payments" or "quarterly payments.")
- **Collateral**—("The portfolio of loans.")
- **Personal Guarantors**—("None." Still, you need to expect that a third-party lender will want you to guarantee the loan.)
- Again, all things are negotiable, so if he balked at "none," you could say, "Well, that's just something I'm really not prepared to do. But let's talk about some of the other items. I would be willing to discuss the interest rate."
- I might then hear: "In that case, we'll charge you 12 percent instead of 9 percent."

It's impossible for me to give you the "best terms" to list on the sheet. I can tell you that very soon after you present this to a lender or two, you will get a feel for what is doable for your portfolio, in your town, with your bankers.

Trust me: Your even having this comprehensive loan proposal will speak volumes about your professionalism. Later, don't be surprised if you hear comments along the lines of, "Bill, you know that loan proposal you sent us on your first deal? I've never seen anything so detailed and professional in my 21 years in the banking business."

### Relationship with Lender

If you have accounts, mortgages, or credit cards with the bank, list those facts. I don't mean account numbers, but just the general facts about your relationship, including how long it's been going on.

### Credit Report

Until you establish a regular borrowing relationship with this bank for these types of loans, you should always include your credit report, regardless of whether it's a positive report or an ugly one.

If it is positive, you want the banker to be able to see your credit report and for *him* to know that *you* know what your credit report says. You have demonstrated to him that your credit is important to you and that you are reasonably sophisticated. You know how to measure and monitor your credit. If I'm a banker, you've just earned some brownie points.

Don't get me wrong: He'll still pull your credit report, because he wants to ensure that what he's looking at is authentic. But put it in the loan package both as a convenience and to show that you know the game.

Now let's say you have a negative report, whether due to late payments, foreclosures, tax liens, or other items. Not only should you include that report, but take out a highlighter and highlight all the negatives! Do it even if you must mark up the whole page.

Then, behind your credit report, include a page with one paragraph titled: "Explanation and Lesson Learned." Make it only one paragraph long. Do not make excuses, do not rationalize, and do not point fingers. Bankers have heard them all and they only reflect poorly on you.

In my case, it was really simple to write:

In 1986 I was in the oil and gas pipe supply business. The price of oil went from $40 a barrel to $14 a barrel within about a week. My business suffered accordingly. I learned not to be involved in politically unstable businesses.

This one paragraph explained everything on my credit report. I didn't blame OPEC or cry in my beer. I also certainly did not try to hide it or pretend they'd never bother to look. I did not say to myself, "If they think it's important, they'll let me know."

The guy processing your application hates surprises. He thought you were a nice enough fellow. But if he opens your credit report and it's a disaster area—and you never alerted him about it—you've just misled him by omission.

Now you not only have a lousy credit report, but you also dinged your own reputation by trying to ignore it.

Do not omit it from the loan proposal and try to explain it verbally to him. How can you be sure he'll adequately relay your explanation to the other loan decision makers?

It's far better to be out in front of bad news when you're trying to convince someone. Yet again it sets you apart from 99 percent of the people this loan officer will ever deal with.

When you're sitting with the loan officer, you'll briefly go through the entire report. When you reach the tab with the credit report, simply say, "This is my credit report and I've highlighted all the things that you probably ought to have an interest in and yes, there's a bunch of them. I explained it all in the one paragraph after the report."

If he wants to ask you questions about it, he'll ask.

### Board of Advisors

This is very important. You leverage your ability to solve future problems by the people with whom you surround yourself. The banker knows that you're new to the loan business. What if you encounter problems that are unfamiliar to you? What will you do?

If you have a circle of people in whom you can confide and ask for help, it's far better than having to say, "Gosh, I don't know."

These advisors could include your attorney, accountant, and other professionals. They might include a businessperson you know from the Chamber of Commerce or from a local charity you support. Get creative about whom you know.

You're not asking these people to be your daily coaches. You merely want their permission to list their names and call them from time to time with questions. Successful people will think even more highly of you for creating this group.

### Significant Professional Relationships
To the extent that you have not already mentioned relationships with professionals like your attorney, then this would be a good place to do so.

### Acknowledgments
If you have things you're proud of, this is not the place to be modest. Be honest and factual. You're providing reasons for the lender to think: "This is the kind of upstanding citizen we like to have as a customer of our bank."

### Financial Statements
This is similar advice to what I gave you in the Credit Report discussion. Simply provide the cover statement of your tax return here. There is no need to provide all of the backup schedules. Include tax returns for both your personal and business entities.

### Business Plan
I covered this subject in an earlier chapter. You can say here "Please see attached."

### Sample Employee Handbook
I would say here "Please see attached" and include one.

I know what you're thinking: "Bill, I'm going to look a little silly as a one-person shop with an 'employee handbook.'"

My advice is counterintuitive but it works. The banker sitting across from you will think the same thing you did: "Well, this is superfluous. He doesn't need that. He has the cart way in front of the horse." As soon as he says that to himself, he'll then think: "I wish all my customers had the cart and the horse out there."

You have just demonstrated to him what a forward-thinking person you are, and that's always a positive in a lending relationship. The last thing a borrower or a banker wants is for you to be surprised by success. If you're surprised about anything occurring in your business, the outcome is likely to be bad. Instead, you have shown him that you are anticipating success.

I don't suggest that you beat your chest and proclaim: "Watch—we're going to be the largest company in the whole wide world!" Simply keep it as a factual item that's listed at the end of the loan proposal and it will serve to impress most loan officers.

You may wonder what to put in this handbook. Because this is a book about buying bad loans and not about employee management, I don't have room to include it here. I have a sample employee handbook you can download from my site at www.RoadToMajor Wealth.com at no charge by typing the word "handbook" in the search box.

### Training Manual

This is the same story as with the employee handbook, for the same reasons. When you go to the web site I just referred you to, you can download one of these, too. Just type "training" into the search box.

## Mechanics

This document should look as impressive as your business plan. Get it typed up nicely on heavy paper. Make several copies so you can ask the loan officer how many she needs. Do not rely on copy machines to convey your precious message.

Avoid anything cutesy; you're dealing with bankers, remember? Make sure your name and contact information are on the cover.

### Your Secret Weapon for Securing a Loan

Whether you're dealing with a two-party transaction or a three-party one, eventually you will get to the point where the banker is discussing the details of your loan. If you need a little extra octane to make the deal happen, I have just the ticket.

In the world of real estate, there's something called "short sales." It's where the bank can modify the terms of the loan if it perceives that the alternative is to have the borrower go belly-up. The bank doesn't like to do them, but it will regularly do short sales. That's because if it has too many delinquent mortgage loans on its books, bank regulations then limit the number of new loans it can make. New loans equal new fees, and—as we've established—that's the lifeblood of the bank.

News flash: With consumer loans, the bank cannot discount the loan to a borrower in trouble. It simply will not do a discounted settlement with its own customer.

Why is that? Because all hell would break loose if the bank allowed it. Borrowers would pour into the bank, asking for exceptions: "My canary died and I can't pay my full bill." "My astrologer told me not to settle any old debts this month."

> But Bill, you just finished saying that short sales are very common in banking.

Yes, I did—for real estate. You see, the bank sells that real estate paper off to Fannie Mae, Freddie Mac, or another institution before the ink is dry on the contract. It can then say to the delinquent borrower, "Hey, we'll see what we can do about a short sale but we're not in the driver's seat on this. Your loan is actually with Fannie Mae in Washington."

On the other hand, your consumer loan for that chemical tank stays locally with that bank. There's no Fannie Mae-type outfit for that paper to be sold to. Therefore, the bank does not want to establish a precedent of listening to excuses for why borrowers can't pay.

In you walk, wanting to buy those bad debts from the bank. When you own them, you can do whatever you please with those debts in terms of discounting them, altering the interest rates, and so on.

You will have flexibility that the bank will never have. That flexibility may be just the thing some borrowers need to get back on track with payments. Then if someone says to the bank, "Hey, how come you gave Bob Jones a break on his chemical tank loan? I'm his brother and you're not helping me out on my loan."

The bank can say: "We'd love to help you, but it's out of our hands. We sold a portfolio of loans including Bob's to a buyer, and Bob arranged that discount with the buyer, not with us. Bank policy does not allow us to do that sort of thing."

## Non-Bank Financing Sources

I do suggest that you initially get your financing in two-party transactions, where the seller finances your purchase of his paper. Then I recommend you branch out to three-party transactions, where a bank finances your purchase of another entity's paper.

A variation of that theme is where a non-bank finances your purchases of portfolios. It's very common in the real estate world, where there's such a thing as a *hard-money lender*. It could be a person or a company. In either case, this lender does not care about the credit rating (or lack thereof) of the borrower.

The lender also does not care about the inexperience of the borrower. Instead, the lender looks at the property the borrower wants financed. If that property has plenty of value versus the loan amount, then the lender may agree to the loan. If this new borrower defaults on the loan, the hard-money lender gets to keep the property.

Down the road, you might find just such lenders to finance your portfolios. They will look at the underlying loans and make their own determination of collectability. Then if you do not pay, they'd own the portfolio. It's not as desirable a lending source as a bank, because hard-money interest rates are often exorbitant. But it's another option for you to have in the right circumstances.

The same is true with "private placements," where you raise money from multiple investors. They pay you fees and allow you to use their money in order to buy a portfolio of loans. You then repay their investment plus some agreed-upon profit.

Private placement arrangements are complicated to set up. They most definitely are not something you can learn out of a book and create yourself, no matter how sophisticated you think you are. When you get to the point that you need millions of dollars in funding, it will be worth your while to hire an experienced securities attorney and accountant to advise you on these advanced structures.

## In the Next Chapter

Not only are you now the proud owner of a portfolio of loans, but it's 100 percent financed. I hope you realize how far you've come in this business. You are deeply into something which few people have the slightest idea about.

That's good for us—it keeps the competition down. Now it's time to turn all this work into money by contacting borrowers. It's the best part of the business, as you will soon see.

CHAPTER

8

# How to Manage Your Portfolio

**E**arlier I said that you lock in your profit when you establish a price for your portfolio and buy it from the seller. It's only a *paper profit* at that point. Now comes the process of turning that paper profit into real money you can enjoy.

You bought that portfolio of loans and got it financed. You're now back at your kitchen table. What's next?

## The Mindset of a Bill Collector

I can just see you recoiling at the words "bill collector." It's become a pretty powerful term in our society, hasn't it? Unfortunately, it is powerful for the wrong reasons. I saw something recently in *USA Today* to the effect that the #1 complaint received by state attorneys general is not car dealer problems, or little old ladies being conned out of their life savings; the #1 complaint is bill collectors.

It made me shake my head: Some of the industry hasn't changed in the many years since I got into it.

As I mentioned in an early chapter, I was the victim of bill collectors for many years when I was poor and when businesses I owned went under. I'm not qualified to examine my own personality dispassionately and tell you exactly what motivated me at different times. But I can tell you that when I had that first box of loans from the bank, and I was about to make that first collection call, I was damned if I would treat borrowers the way bill collectors treated me.

I very quickly realized I was on to something:

- I collected more than I thought I would
- It was not a confrontational experience with the borrowers, which meant that . . .
- . . . I was not burned out at the end of my calls.

I can say with some confidence that you really didn't know what you were getting yourself into when you picked up this book. If you've been exposed to the bill collection industry, you must have thought this book might provide insights into the seedy side of the industry.

## Mean Does Not Pay

Well, the industry may still harbor a large number of seedy characters, but you and I don't need to be associated with them. The extremely good news for us is I learned that Mean Does Not Pay. Oh, when you bully people, a certain number of them will comply. But early on, I realized there was a phenomenon at work that could make me far wealthier than your average bill collector.

You'll probably agree with me that many consumers are not just behind on one bill. It may start out that way, but soon they are way behind on multiple bills. Whether it's due to bad relationships, being fired from their jobs, poor health, or a hundred other reasons, it's almost as if people just throw in the towel at some point and stop caring about *all* their obligations.

That means they may have two or three dozen creditors hounding them at one time. Here's where it gets very interesting: What if you were the single bill collector who treated them like human beings? What if your true operating principle was to show dignity and respect to the people who owed you money?

I can tell you for a fact what happens: If they have any money at all to put toward paying down some of their bills, they'll pay yours first.

This is not theory cooked up by some professor who wants to publish a paper. It's the result of my 39 years in business and 12 years in the collection industry. It's the result of dealing with $15 billion in loans from 800 financial institutions, involving 4.5 million borrowers. And it's what made me a billionaire.

I'd like to tell you that I built this oasis of professionalism because I was motivated by some spiritual guidance. That was not the case. When I built my company I was not very much involved in religion at all.

No, my motivation was good old American capitalism: I found a way to become so head-and-shoulders better than my bill-collecting competition that the strange sound they heard was all the companies dumping them and signing up with me. I had relationships with 21 of the top 25 banks in America, not because they liked me as a person. We worked together because my professional approach meant they would not receive bad publicity.

With 3,900 employees, you can imagine that it is a challenge to get them all to fly in formation. People are people. Therefore, I had to get serious about certain ironclad rules if I wanted to grow the business and maintain our great reputation at the same time.

## Offenses That Would Get You Fired on the Spot

We had the standard rules about excessive tardiness, drugs in the workplace, and so on. But the thing that made us different from the rest of the industry was this: If you raised your voice, uttered profanities, threatened or intimidated customers—you were fired on the spot. After one single violation.

People took me seriously after my best friend and drinking buddy came in one day and violated one of the principles. I fired him immediately, and word got around that the Old Man meant it.

We really tried to hire people with very different backgrounds, but we were totally inflexible on one point: If you had any previous experience in the debt collection industry, you were ineligible to work at my company.

It was like trying to re-train vicious pit bulls to become sweet dogs around kids. Could it be done? Sure, with enough time and money. I was on a mission to grow very quickly, and simply could not afford to become a shelter for those poor souls.

When we hired new employees, we would tell them:

"We want you to treat people with dignity and respect. We want you to be nice to them, and work with them. We want you to be empathetic and really understand what's going on in their life. The more you know about people, the more you'll be able to help them, and the more successful our company will be."

The employee would be like, "Yeah, um, sure. No problem." Translated, that meant: "Okay, you can count on me to spout the corporate B.S. line, just like my previous company treated their employees like garbage while their lobby had a big sign that read: "Our People Are Our Greatest Asset."

We got that incoming attitude not from former bill collectors, but from just regular employees. They soon realized we were not kidding when they saw people fired for one single infraction.

Within the constraints of the law, you're of course free to run your business however you see fit. You would be very smart—and quite a bit richer—if you run it by treating your customers with dignity and respect.

Let's now dive in and prepare your new portfolio to make you some money.

## Organize Your Loans

If you haven't already done so, I suggest you start a spreadsheet to capture all the information you'll be collecting. It's what I used for years before we got really big and had annual technology budgets of more than $100 million.

Start small at first with name of borrower and contact information. You'll be adding columns for status notes like "bankruptcy," "dead," and so on. Simply start small for now.

The first sort order you should use is *highest dollar of collectability*. Maybe your best estimated cash recovery was $15,000, so that one is at the top. Then you have one loan for $10,000, several for $9,000, and so on, down to the ones that are graded zero at the bottom of the list.

You now know your priority accounts. They are where you should be focusing your effort and energy. You clearly want to get to know those top people, because if you can collect them, you won't need to collect the ones on the bottom. It's the *80-20 Rule:* You should spend 80 percent of your time and money on the 20 percent of accounts that will give you the very most return. Besides, the sooner you collect from those top accounts, the sooner you'll have paid back your loan and will be in the profit zone.

After doing this spreadsheet and sorting process, your next step is to decide how many accounts you will pull a credit report on. Don't pull reports for the bottom of your list, because it will not be cost-effective. Just pick some cutoff for now. You can readjust later.

There may be some other bits of information to gather on accounts as you scan the list. Remember that you most likely bought a box of local loans. That means local people.

The day I bought that very first package of loans, I stopped to have lunch in Tulsa at Bill and Ruth's Submarine Shop. I had a standard sandwich and went to the bank for my closing. I was reviewing the files again briefly and stopped. I'd seen that name somewhere before: "Bill and Ruth." I had just eaten in their sandwich shop.

As the new owner of that loan, I now had useful additional information. They were store owners still actively in business. I didn't even need to pull a credit report on them in order to begin the collection process.

This sort of thing doesn't happen very often but it does happen. You don't need too many of these lucky breaks to add up to several very collectable loans. Therefore, keep your eyes open for opportunities to drive by an address to see what's going on there.

## Be Prepared for the Call

Do not call up customers and be unprepared for the conversation. The more information you have about them prior to picking up that telephone, the more effective you will be.

Consider the first impression you leave if you start the conversation this way:

> Hey, John, my name is Bill Bartmann and I bought your loan here and let me—hang on, hang on one second here, yeah, it looks like it was a car loan, a Ford, did you buy a Ford?

You just exposed your ignorance and the customer already knows that you don't know. On the other hand, what impression do you leave if you start the conversation this way:

> Hi, John, my name is Bill Bartmann and I bought your loan from Bank of Commerce. It was your car loan, your 1942 Ford—the blue one. Remember that one?

You now remember more about this car than the customer probably does. Before you pick up the phone, do the research you think is appropriate for the size of the balance and the collectability, based on your spreadsheet.

Part of that familiarization is reading the credit report. It contains a ton of useful information. Train yourself to draw conclusions from it, the way Sherlock Holmes would. For instance, you might look at the report and think: "Okay, John owes five other people money and he's not paying any of them."

Then you see in another part of the file that his wife's name is Sally and he's got three kids named Johnny, Timmy, and Gertrude. John tells you on the phone, "Well, Bill, my wife left me and my girl's been sick." You could say, "John, when did Susie leave you and how's Gertrude doing now?"

I can tell you, it's amazingly powerful. And what did it cost you? A few moments of preparation to look down and get a sense of John's relationships and situation.

> But Bill, we all know what the collection industry is like. Your company may have been different, but most people despise bill collectors who call. Even if I'm the nicest person in the world, that customer doesn't know that. How do you keep them on the phone long enough to realize you're not like the rest of those people?

We had a standard script that we refined over the course of collecting on literally millions of customers. The account officers memorized it during their seven-week training program. The script was as follows:

> "Hi John, my name is Bill Bartmann and I'm with Commercial Financial Services here in Tulsa and we recently purchased your
> *(continued)*

> (*continued*)
> loan from the Bank of Commerce and it shows here the balance outstanding at the present time is $10,372. John, what can we do about that?"

The script just ended. That was the totality of the script.

Now you shut up and listen. John's about to tell you something.

Let's say that John is not in a good mood today, and he says to you, "Go to hell."

You then say:

> Well, John, I'd like to work with you on this. I'd like to find a way to take care of this in a form or fashion that makes good sense for you.
>
> I think you know that I don't need to collect 100 cents on the dollar out of this thing, but I do need to get some satisfaction. So what *could* you do?

Now you've already said something that no one else has said to John. You just offered him a discount. I usually don't like starting off by talking about a discount. On the other hand, if John begins with a "Go to hell," I can guess the next sound I will hear is the dial tone.

> Bill, what if we don't even get that far, and as soon as they hear, "I'm with Commercial Financial Services. I bought your loan . . ." I hear click—dial tone?

I will not lie to you. That does happen with a percentage of the population. Under the Fair Debt Collection Practices Act, you have limitations on how many times you can call back before it becomes harassment. You can find a link to that set of regulations on my web site at www.RoadToMajorWealth.com, by going to the search box and typing in the word "rules." I strongly suggest you read it, because you will be subject to it.

Back to John's account: If you call back right away, all you're going to do is make John mad. If you make him mad, you lose. Remember, you're trying to collect on a loan that several other people tried to collect on, and were uniformly unsuccessful.

It's much better to wait until John calms down. That might be the next day. Then call him back and say, "Hey, John, before you hang up. . . ." Notice that John doesn't even know who this is yet. So start with:

> Hey, John, before you hang up, please don't hang up on me, just give me 30 seconds to talk to you. Could you do that? Would that be okay?

Here's the cool thing that happens after a while: You have heard every objection by John that he could ever make. You don't have a long, planned script. Instead, you let John determine what the next move is. For instance, I just showed you how to handle the person who greets you with "Go to hell."

If you instead reached Ruth at Bill and Ruth's Submarine Shop, she might be having a better day than John was having. She might be civil. So when you give her the standard script ending in: ". . . Ruth, what can we do about that?" she might come back with: "Well, there's just no way on earth I can pay off that ten grand, but the bank told me it was 'pay it all or see you in court.'"

In that case, you have a live one on your hands. You just determined that Ruth might be a good candidate for a payment plan.

If you want to get some practice before starting in on your highest-value accounts, then start at the bottom. At my company, we would give the low-ECR accounts to our training department.

They were real people who owed real money to us. Our trainees would practice on them and the consequence of failure was minimal.

## Settlements to Shoot For

After you get comfortable with making calls, you should work your highest-value accounts first. When you work them, don't just cave in and settle for a few dollars right up front. Instead here's what you want to shoot for, in the following order.

1. *Ask for all of it.*

    Remember, you will never get more than what you ask for. If you start off asking for less than the face value of the loan you bought, it will always be less. But when your very first conversation starts with "Ruth, you owe me $10,564. . . . What can we do about that?", you have just essentially asked Ruth for all of it.

2. *Suggest a discounted settlement.*

    That's where you might say to Ruth, "I have great news for you. Because I'm the owner of the loan and the bank no longer has any say in the matter, I think we can work something out that's less than the full $10,564. What could you swing?" Let Ruth give you a number. If you give her a number first, it might be lower than what she had in mind.

3. *Suggest a payment plan.*

    "Ruth, I still want you to owe me $10,564 but I'll take it in installments instead of all of it at one time. What could you pay per month?"

## The Two Main Approaches That Set You Apart

We all know that most bill collectors have the reputation of browbeating people and intimidating them until either they get paid or they give up. I suggest that you take two approaches, both of which are very different from the conventional model:

## "Can't Do Nothing" Approach

Remember the "Go to hell" response? Let's say you got a polite variation of that from Tony, after you ended your script with "Tony, what can we do about that?" Let's say he said, "Well, nothing. I'm flat broke."

Whereupon Tony would proceed to tell you just how broke he was, and all the things that were going on in his life. You should take detailed notes and then say:

> Tony, the only thing we *can't* do is "nothing," and you're asking me to do nothing. So we've gotta come up with something.
>
> So, Tony, tell me again what can you do? Are you still working at Ajax Manufacturing?

You can throw in that last tidbit about Tony because you saw it in his file. If Tony says, "No, the jerks fired me," you say, "Oh, what happened?"

Tony will tell you because he's that kind of a guy. You'll listen carefully for details about his situation, but no matter what he says, you get around to saying, "Well, Tony, what can we do about this?"

That is because you're prepared to listen, but you're not prepared for a song-and-dance that leads to nothing. We can't do nothing. That is one of those logical arguments that Tony can't win. He can yell, call you names, and hang up—and some people will do all three—but he can't win on the merits of *doing nothing* about his loan.

## Hall-Pass Approach

The *hall pass* is when you say: "Well, Tony, what can we do about this?" and Tony replies:

> Oh, Bill, I just can't do anything right now because I lost my job, my wife left me, my car broke down, and my huntin' dog died.

You should not laugh, giggle, or groan. Just listen quietly and write down everything Tony just said. If you conclude that he has some willingness but inability to pay right now, then say:

> Tony, wow, man, your life is really not going very good right now, is it, buddy? Wow, that's bad. I'm sorry to hear that. Hey, Tony, here's what I want to do. You've got some stuff going in your life and you really do need to deal with that, and I'm not the biggest fish in your barrel right now. You need to take care of some of your other problems.
>
> Why don't I just make a note here that I'll call you back in 60 days, and why don't you take the next 60 days to try and go sort that stuff out. *(Be explicit about what the stuff is, as in finding a new job, getting his car fixed, and so on.)*
>
> Man, I hope you can find a job and I really wish you luck with that. I'm not gonna call you back for 60 days. So good luck and Tony, take care of yourself, okay?

You hang up after he mumbles some agreement.

Exactly 60 days from today you're calling Tony back. Not 59 days, and not 61 days. Why? Because you are keeping your word. You want to create a relationship with Tony where keeping one's word is important. You've got to demonstrate it first. If you expect Tony to keep his word and you don't keep yours, this will not last long.

On the 60th day, you call.

Tony, hi, this is Bill Bartmann. Remember 60 days ago we talked and you were telling me that you had lost your job over at Ajax Manufacturing. How's that going? Were you able to get a new one?

You're waiting for Tony to tell you. He may say, "Yes, I got a new one and life is great." That does not happen very often. Even if he did find a new job, he may say, "But Susie still left me and my dog is still dead."

Remember that you own that account, and you are in a position to give Tony another hall pass if you think he's being straight with you.

Here's another principle: Whether the hall pass is for another 30 days or another 60 days, make sure it's long enough that Tony thinks you're being generous.

Your intention is to hang up that phone with Tony and have him think "What in the hell just happened? Some bill collector called, he listened to my plight, and he told me he's not gonna call back for 60 days. I don't believe that for a second. I think he's gonna call back tomorrow."

Tony's in disbelief. He's amazed because nobody has ever done that to him. All the other bill collectors have called up saying, "Tony, you deadbeat scum, you owe me $15,844 and if you don't pay, some real bad things are about to happen" or words to that effect.

If Tony is in a position to pay just one of his many delinquent obligations, who do you suppose will get the money?

Bill, are there ever circumstances where you are justified in making a threat?

Never. Period. In my company, it was grounds for instant termination if an account officer raised his voice, issued profanity, or even got confrontational with a customer.

By the way, we specifically used the word "customer." I believe we were the very first people in the industry to think of these people who owed us money as customers. Everyone else called them "deadbeats," "pond scum," "scallywags"—and those were the polite terms. We were on a mission to raise bill collecting out of the gutter and elevate it to the level of helping people.

Do we want to be paid? Absolutely. My 3,900 employees had families to feed, too. But we treated people with dignity and respect for one simple reason: It was good business in an area with an extremely bad reputation. I made the strategic observation that Mean Didn't Pay, and became a billionaire from applying the opposite principles.

We were polite but firm. We emphasized the point that "doing nothing" was not an option. Could borrowers use their imaginations to conclude that we may use all legal means to collect what we were owed? Of course. But it was never a "do this or else" equation. Again, we wanted to get paid first when the customer was deciding between paying a couple dozen overdue bills. To threaten would just stick us back in the group with all other bill collectors.

Bill, what if Tony says, "No I can't pay you anything." and I say, "Well, I'm sorry, but the one thing that we can't do is nothing," and Tony says, "Yeah, you want to see me do nothing?"

You then say:

Well, Tony, let's not even get into that kind of a conversation because that's not gonna take us anywhere. You've got this loan problem and I can be a solution for you. I can actually help you get your credit back.

Now, I can't make you pure as the driven snow and anybody who promises you that is lying through his teeth. But I sure can make this problem become a smaller issue in your life. And I can actually help you turn it into a positive. Would you like to talk about that?

Remember that when you finish talking, you shut up and listen actively. Tony then says, "I don't care no more about my credit. It's shot anyway." Then you say:

Well, Tony, then you're really not giving me hardly any alternatives here and I don't want to even be in that space. So what could we do? Let's talk about your life right now. With the circumstances you're facing and with all the things going on in your world, what *could* you do?

One possible reply from Tony would be: "I couldn't pay you more than 15 cents on the dollar." Now you're making progress—15 cents is now the new "floor" on this discussion, and you can only go up from here. If you only paid Frank Smith 2 or 3 cents for the loan, you should now be smiling inside. You continue:

I'm glad we're talking. That's good news, Tony. Doesn't that feel a little bit better that we're finally communicating?

And you know what? 15 cents isn't crazy. I can't say "yes" to that because that doesn't work for me, because I've got more than that invested in this.

*(What you mean—but don't say—is you paid a lot for the whole loan portfolio, and not just for his loan.)*

*(continued)*

> (*continued*)
>    Tony, I could give you a big discount. I could make this thing go away but I can't do 15 cents. I could probably do 30 cents and if you could find a way to come up with 30 cents I could make 70 cents on the dollar go away. Right now you owe me $10,000. I can give you back $7,000 by discounting down to $3,000.

## People Who Agree Too Quickly

You will come across people who simply want to get you off the phone by agreeing to whatever you say. You reach a specific number in the conversation and they say, "Yeah, yeah fine, okay, I'm sending the check next Monday for sure."

Here again, you need to use your judgment, which will be getting steadily better. If you thought they were only saying that to get you off the phone, say:

> Well, Tony, hang on, buddy. I don't want you to make a promise that you can't keep, okay? So let's talk about what you really can do.
>    "No, no. I can pay it."
>    Tony, if you can, that'd be great and I'd love to get it, but let's not make it hard on you. Let's talk about maybe breaking this into two or three installments. Would that be even easier for you?

Please understand the judgment call here: You offer the installment approach if you don't believe him. You want him to consider you generous.

On the other hand, if you did believe him, you'd say, "Tony, that's great. Terrific. Here's the information you're gonna need. . . ." You would make sure he got your mailing address and other payment details.

If you sensed that he wasn't writing it down, that would tip you off that he did not intend to send it. In that case, you say:

Tony, if you're gonna do that for me—and I really appreciate it—can I ask you to do me a favor right now? (*You're waiting for him to say "yes" or "no." If he says "no," he's not sending you the check. If he says "yes", he probably is sending it to you.*)

Here's what I want you to do and this will really make this so much easier for both of us. I would like you right now to set the phone down, go get your checkbook, and let's write out that check. Don't send it to me yet, but let's write it out right now. Can you do that?

"Well, I told you I'd send it on Monday."

Yeah, but I want to make this really easy for you. If you go write the check right now and you put it in an envelope and put my name and address that I give you—you don't have to put a stamp on it and you don't have to mail it until Monday.

But I think we're both gonna feel a lot better if we know when Monday comes, this is gonna be a done deal. And I'm gonna be tickled to death to be able to report your credit is A-OK, paying as agreed. So could you do that for me?

Based on what he tells you, you'll know whether he's lying through his teeth or not. You can say, "And what was the check number on that, Tony?" I'll save that until the end, because if he doesn't have a check number he's been lying all the time. You say:

Good, then. Would you mind if I called you back Monday just to kind of be a wakeup call?

"No, dammit. I told you I would send it on Monday."

Well, Tony, hey, look, I'm not trying to irritate you. I'm trying to make this problem go away. Are you sure doing this in

(*continued*)

(*continued*)
installments wouldn't be a better deal for you? In fact, why don't
you just make a small first payment?

Now you don't believe a word he's saying, given his responses. You
should try to ease off the size of the payment. You must be perceptive
enough to sense you have just overshot your goal and have to let Tony
partially off the hook, but do it with grace and diplomacy. Here's why:

The Tonys of this world have been in this box before and, yes,
they've had to say things they knew they couldn't do. But after being
in this business a long time, I believe that 90 percent of people are
not morally bankrupt, even though they may be financially bankrupt. When they have to lie to someone because of their financial
circumstances, it hurts them a lot.

If you sense they're already overextending their capacity, back
them up and make them feel good again. Tony thinks: "I told Bill I
would send him all of it, but then he said one-third would be okay,
too, so now I'll be sure to pay him on Monday."

## A Powerful Tactic

You may already have discerned it: My approach was: I'm going to
get you to like me. I'm going to establish rapport with you. I will get
you to not dread my phone call.

Don't misunderstand: I still am getting the message across that
I'm a bill collector and not your drinking buddy. I'm still going to
engage you and not let you blow me off. I'll be persistent, but it's a
win/win persistence: You get to erase significant debt and that helps
to restore your credit; in the meantime, I get a return on my
investment in bad loans.

## You Already Know How to Be an Excellent Collector

You've just never done it for a living. I'm sorry if I have conned
you in a sense: Here you went out and bought a book on how to

make lots of money by investing in bad loans. But the truth is that you already have the fundamental skills built into you. What are those skills?

- Truly listening to people
- Acting interested
- Showing concern for someone else
- Responding appropriately
- Thinking about people's needs and not just demanding that your needs be met
- Being empathetic for a fellow human being who is suffering

Those are the key ingredients in every meaningful relationship we have, whether it be with our spouse, boss, employees, or friends.

We already know how to say: "Oh, man, I'm sorry to hear about that." Or "Gee, Aunt Sally, they took out your kidney? Wow; I bet that hurt." Well, Aunt Sally is thrilled to hear you say those words. That doesn't mean we've ever had a kidney taken out, but she knows we're concerned about her.

Being a good bill collector isn't hard. For instance, it's not as hard as being a plumber. To become a plumber, you need to know lots of technical stuff. You also must be able to operate a torch and many different cutting and joining tools. In the debt collection industry, you're just talking to people.

But Bill, won't I get my brains kicked in? Aren't you asking me to do a job that has more rejection than just about anything else? After all, if I were a car salesman, at least they would come to see me on the lot. As a bill collector, aren't I the last person they want to see—maybe after their ex?

If you were going to ask them for a 100 cents on the dollar, you would be right. If you are like most of the other collectors, who want to be paid all the money owed them, then you're correct.

When you are now the *new* owner of the paper, you have the power to grant them a wonderful gift. Don't start with the attitude of calling them up and making them do something they don't want to do.

Start with the attitude of "Hey, Tony, I bought your debt and I can really help you. I mean it." Will it help Tony if I could forgive a piece of his debt? Absolutely. He'll feel better about a piece of the burden that's been weighing him down.

It can also help his credit report. As the owner of the debt, you have the capacity to report his account status to the credit bureaus. You can't fix his past, but you can report the present.

If you just agreed to settle Tony's $10,000 account for $2,000, you now report to three different agencies that this account has "paid as agreed," or "settled as agreed," or is "payment plan satisfactory." There are many different terms.

If you report Tony as *paid as agreed*, creditors looking at his credit bureau report will not know that Tony paid you only a fraction of the face value. They'll just know that as a creditor, you are satisfied.

That's powerful when Tony is in the market for a new car. He may have other dings on his report, but you're helping to make that report show some promise. The car dealer may convince himself that this Tony fellow is taking steps to turn his credit around; he "paid as agreed" to you.

### Be Sure to Get Testimonials

Get this: We had literally thousands of glowing "thank you" letters. They were written by people from whom we had collected money, that no one else had ever collected from!

Do you fathom the power of that? When a banker wants to see proof of your reputation, you pull out the letters. When the occasional complaining customer calls the Better Business Bureau because he does not want *anyone* to ask him to pay his debts, you pull out those letters. If your experience is like mine, you'll never get a call again from the Better Business Bureau. They'll know you're one of the very few Good Guys.

Here's what you should do: When you have successfully collected on an account, ask for a testimonial letter. Say:

> Hey, Tony, I know we just agreed to settle your account for 30 cents on the dollar and I appreciate that. I'll be glad to get your check.
>
> Would you do me one more favor, please? Would you scribble me a short note? I don't care if you do it with a ballpoint pen on a Big Chief pad, or type it up, or e-mail it. Whatever you feel comfortable with. Tony, I would very much like to have a note in my file of your comments on how this transaction worked for you. Would you mind?

You just settled the account for a 70 percent discount. Of course, he's going to write you a letter. Please note that I didn't tell Tony what to write.

We also got plenty of unsolicited letters from customers. But we got a lot more great stories when we simply started asking them to jot down their experience with us. It's an extremely valuable tool you can use to make your financing and public-relations life go as smoothly as possible.

## To Sue or Not to Sue

You may find this hard to believe, but in more than 4.5 million completed collection cases, we never sued anyone. Not one person.

Was it because I was such a nice, friendly guy? No, it was a calculated business decision based on three factors.

First, remember the borrowers I was dealing with: They had resisted the heaviest-duty hard-core collection techniques by firms that preceded me. I couldn't see how I would be more effective in my collections if I had a different piece of paper. The one I had, which said the borrowers were legally obligated to pay me, was called a *contract*. The one I'd get if I won the lawsuit would be called a *judgment*. Would that label really make any difference?

Second, I made a return-on-investment decision. Would I spend more time and money chasing this person through the courtroom than I'd get in cash? That calculation almost never made sense.

Third, I was taking a much longer view. Early on I could see that for us to be long-term players, we had to be remarkably different from our competitors.

I knew we would not just encounter the financial considerations of a bank selling us loans, but also the political considerations. It was extremely powerful for me to be able to say to a banker, "In all the loans we've ever done, we have never sued anybody." You could just see the relief wash over his face as he signed the loan sales contract.

Of those three considerations, you and I certainly share the first two. But we don't necessarily share the third, political one. You may just buy one portfolio and decide this business is not for you. You might buy a few portfolios as a sideline, but never as the main focus of your business.

If that's your situation, then you might very well conclude that it's time to sue a customer. Make sure you're doing it not out of "I'll show him!" anger, but for rational investment reasons.

Nevertheless, if you do end up in a position where you want to be a long-term player in this extraordinarily profitable business, you might heed that third reason I gave.

## How Many Calls Does It Take?

It's possible to be successful with collections on the first call. Remember that we're blowing people away with the different approach we're taking to collections, and sometimes they respond right away.

As a general rule, though, we had a longer process. It could happen all in one phone call, as I said. However, we would encourage it not to happen in one phone call. We wanted to tell them the good news that a new and better company owned their loan, and that we had flexibility that the prior owner did not have.

We wanted to give them a little time between calls to absorb that information. We would then call them back in the agreed number of days. People tend to react better when they're not surprised and when you've built up at least a tiny relationship with them.

Stated another way, I would encourage you to ask politely for the full balance in the first phone call using the script I already gave you.

If Tony says "No, I can't" for whatever reason, don't even offer the other two settlement options yet.

You should see where the conversation is heading. The sophisticated and successful poker players don't play *their* hand. They play *your* hand. You must be ready to play Tony's hand by what he's telling you, and how he said it.

Listen to Tony. Based on what he says, if you conclude that he's never going to take your call again if you don't move to *phase two*, then move there on that first call. To refresh your memory, *phase two* is the offer of a discounted settlement. *Phase three* is the offer of a payment plan.

## Bill, can I be prohibited from calling some customers?

Yes, you can. First, you must realize that I'm not giving you legal advice. I have no idea where you live, and the current rules in your state are the ones you must follow, not to mention federal laws.

Borrowers can invoke a *cease and desist* rule. It doesn't happen when they say "Leave me alone" or "Don't ever call me again!"

It is only activated when borrowers send you a letter that tells you to cease and desist. They must communicate that to you in a manner other than verbally.

Even so, we were always very careful, given the cooperative approach we wanted to establish with customers. Therefore, if a customer did not write us a letter, but merely uttered the "leave me alone" concept, we had a special department handle all future calls. Only people from our legal department would be allowed to make future calls.

If you're a one-person shop, your situation will be different. Just be sensitive to the goal of collecting money through a constructive relationship, and let that guide your efforts.

## Leaving Voice Mail Messages

If you get the customer's voice mail, I recommend that you always leave a message. I know that sounds contrary to common advice, but remember who you are: You're not embarrassed and not ashamed. You won't yell and scream; you're here to help.

> Hey, Tony, Bill Bartmann from CFS. I know you're not going to like hearing this, but I bought your debt from Bank of Commerce and I'd like to visit with you.
>
> I know this is just one of those awkward times in life. Please trust me. I'm not going to beat you around the head and shoulders. I just want to talk to you so here's my cell phone number and my office number.
>
> Please let me know when it'd be convenient for me to talk to you—and I'm talking about *your* convenience, not *my* convenience.
>
> So if you give me a call I can make this a very pleasant experience for both of us. Please give me a call.

The size of the account balance will dictate the number of calls you make to Tony.

## Sending Letters

This can be effective when you've tried the phone repeatedly and had no success. Also, if you get a *cease and desist letter* about making no further phone calls, you can only legally contact that customer in two remaining ways—by letter or by lawsuit. We've already discussed the lawsuit angle.

Your letter would simply be the same approach I've shown you above, but written on paper. There's no different "secret sauce" to apply to the letter.

I do recommend that you send the letter using first-class mail. Have it hand-addressed with a normal stamp and a street return address; not a post-office box. Here's why:

- When a piece of first-class mail is undeliverable, you will get it back with the last-known forwarding address the post office has on record. For the price of a stamp, you've just had the post office help you in your skip-tracing efforts. You will not get that service with cheaper forms of mail.

- Having the letter hand-addressed means it will get opened. Do you personally ever throw away such letters? Neither will your customer.

- Do not put the name of your business on the letter. You're not impressing or intimidating anyone by doing that. Instead, you're signaling to the customer "Just another lousy bill collector," at which point you go into the kitchen drawer at best, but more likely into the garbage.

We even used Federal Express when the dollar amount warranted it. For a few bucks, you know for sure that your message was delivered and read on the spot. Keep this approach in mind for the relatively high-value customers.

Needless to say, you must always keep detailed notes concerning each contact you make, whether by phone or letter. It will be how you piece together the clues about what makes this customer tick, and how best to find a solution that involves paying you.

## Always Keep ROI in Mind

That's your *return on investment* calculation, which I've mentioned more than once. Don't get mad with a borrower. Don't get even. Just go get another loan from the portfolio. You should be in this business to be highly efficient, highly profitable, and to go home to your family at the end of the day with a smile on your face. You do that by knowing when it's time to move on.

## Hiring a Collection Agency

If I've done my job in this chapter so far, you're likely to be pleasantly surprised: This bill-collection business is not about knocking someone to the ground, putting your foot on his neck, and extracting his wallet. It's about finding someone who's already on the ground and giving him a helping hand.

I do hope that you at least give the business a try, so you can speak from experience when you eventually delegate the phone work to someone else. I think you'll find the experience rewarding.

Still, your life may currently be such that you simply cannot afford to make phone calls. Perhaps your work and home situation make it very difficult. Maybe you just would rather not bother. You would prefer to give up a portion of the profits in exchange for someone else doing the customer contact.

You do have the option of hiring a collection agency to handle this piece of the equation. Of course, I've just spent many pages describing how most of the industry is inefficient and dumb: They beat up customers, who then become determined never to pay if they can possibly help it. These firms are dumb for not realizing there's a much more profitable way.

The typical collection agency is not a pretty sight: The industry average for employee turnover is commonly 100 percent *per year*, and as high as 200 percent. Is it any wonder that employees burn out after a year of pounding on the guy on the other end of the phone, hour after hour, month after month?

Our employee turnover rate was 9 percent. Our wages were double the industry average. We had full-time daycare on site for all the parents who worked in our company.

One time I decided to throw a little weekend party at Disney World for all our employees and their families. That was over 5,000 people and we all worked in Tulsa. So I rented every Boeing 747 jumbo jet that was available in the free world to have an airlift from Tulsa to Orlando. That would be 27 jumbo jets. It literally was the largest airlift since the Berlin Wall was established. It cost me $12 million, but do you think I got just a little boost in company morale and productivity from it?

Enough about me. The current discussion is about how you can find the best collection agency to handle your portfolio. Where to start?

## How to Find a Good Agency

Just as there are 26 different medical specialties, all of which can be called "M.D.," there are collection agency specialties. Some only do commercial real estate loans, or residential loans. Others only do consumer paper. Your first task is to find the type of agency that matches the portfolio you own.

If you bought a national package of loans from a broker, then you might look at a larger, national firm. The downside of doing so is that you are likely to be a very small fish in a big company. You'll pay more for the service and will be on the bottom rung of their attentiveness ladder. You'll still be on the ladder, though, and that may be what you need to do at first.

Assuming you bought a portfolio of loans from your local banker, then your first step is to determine whom the bank used for collections.

Wait a minute, Bill: You know that the bank used several local agencies. I just bought a portfolio of loans that both the bank and those agencies were unsuccessful collecting on. Why should I use *them?*

Hold your horses! I didn't say "use them," did I? I said find out who they are, so you *do not* use them.

You can find out by looking in the loan files, where you'll probably see letterhead, reports, and memo paper from the collection agencies. If you do not see that, simply ask the banker who sold you the loans.

Now open the phone book. Ignore the collection agencies that advertise a specialty that does not reflect your loan portfolio.

Now you're down to ten agencies. Cross off the three agencies the bank used that were ineffective. Now pick up the phone and call the first remaining one:

Hi, my name is Bill Bartmann and I have a portfolio of loans. They're all consumer paper (*or whatever is in your portfolio*). On average they have a balance of $4,700.

First, would you even be interested in collecting these for me?

If they say "no," all the other questions don't matter. If they say "yes," then say:

Oh, good. Have you ever done this before? And would you have a list of references—some people I might be able to chat with regarding the services you performed for them?

If they've done it before, they should have references. If they don't have references to give you, that's a deal-killer and you politely end the conversation.

Go through your list and narrow it down to the semi-finalists by doing what I suggest above. Now it's time to call references.

> But Bill, don't people only put down references that are favorable to them? What good will that do me?

You do like to ask direct questions of me, don't you? Well, the direct answer is that you will not get any useful information if you ask useless questions. Don't say:

> Hey, Mrs. Jones, my name's Bill Bartmann. I see you sent some accounts over to Ajax Collection Company. Is that true?
> Yes, Mr. Bartmann, it is.
> Did they do a pretty good job for you?
> Yeah, they did a pretty good job for me.
> Okay, thank you.

That just wasted everyone's time. The trick with getting references of any kind for any purpose—whether it be for bill collectors, employees, or whomever—is to get them talking. Just ask normal, commonsense questions:

- Say, how many accounts did you send over?
- Without giving away trade secrets, can you give me a ballpark of how much they were able to collect on your accounts?
- What general percentage did they recover for you?
- How long did that take?

- Did you ever have any problems with them?
- Did they ever get any complaints from any of your accounts?
- Did you ever hear of any allegations or violations of the Fair Debt Collection Practices Act?
- Is there anything they did that you wish they hadn't done?
- What's the nicest thing you could say about them?

Remember that you don't know this reference. You'll never meet him again, so don't try to make it a popularity contest. Just ask your direct questions.

If they give you good answers, that's super. If the answers are so-so, or they beat around the bush, a red flag should go up. If they don't have the time to answer a handful of questions—and they were given as a current reference—that is not a good sign.

I now go to the next reference for this collection agency. I then repeat for the other agencies on my list.

After calling references, contact the Better Business Bureau. You can either do that online or by phone. You might even get more information online, because you're not the hundredth caller today for some overworked person.

You are looking for both complaint history and number of *open* complaints, meaning they have not been resolved. They'll tell you.

Next, contact the Attorney General's office. Every state has one. They're certainly reachable by phone, and now all of them are likely to be online. You might have to find the Consumer Protection Department, or a similar department name. Then ask the very same question you asked the Better Business Bureau: "I'm contemplating doing some business with Ajax Collection Agency in Tulsa, Oklahoma. I just want to know if you've ever had any complaints."

They'll not hesitate to tell you.

---

Bill, what if I go through the whole list of seven and they're all lousy?

That's a possibility. In that case, you must widen your search to surrounding areas until you find a company with a good reputation. On my web site I have a list of collection agencies. You can go to www.RoadToMajorWealth.com, put into the search box the term "collection agency," and get the list from there.

## Stay Local Whenever Possible

Although it's possible to hire a large, national firm to do collections for you, that should not be your first choice. There are very good reasons for staying local:

- Most cities have commonly known zones with distinct styles. For instance, where I live in Tulsa, there are four distinct demographics: South Tulsa is very affluent. North Tulsa is predominantly African American. West Tulsa is an ethnic mix, including blue-collar and no-collar. East Tulsa is becoming predominantly Hispanic.

- If I'm a collector and I see that someone's address is in a subdivision with million-dollar homes, might that be useful information? If you really want to get detailed, might I use a collector of a specific ethnicity to contact customers of a specific ethnicity?

- Local collectors will study the local newspapers and know all about layoffs, plant closings, and new employers coming into town. This is all useful intelligence when talking with customers.

It's unlikely that a national firm will know Tulsa the way a good local company does. Of course, if you get to the stage that you've outgrown the local collection resources, you'll be forced to go to regional or national firms. Then again, you might just build your own good, controllable staff the way I did.

## What to Pay Collection Agencies

Industry standard is thought of as $33\frac{1}{3}$ percent of the gross amount recovered. You should not pay much more than that. However, don't expect much of a discount if you're new to the business and walking in with one small portfolio.

Don't sweat the percentages. You're having this company do the work, remember? You sit back and get profits. Yes, you will pay more at first, but that can quickly change as you grow. When you get to your tenth box, you might be at 25 percent and on the road to getting even 20 percent if you have decent volume. It's no different from working with thousands of other vendors like printers, painters, and programmers.

Heads Up: You should never, ever allow any agency to stick "add-ons" to that percentage. Also there should be no minimum monthly payment or long-term contract. The percentage is the percentage.

## Trust but Verify

Surprise! There are unscrupulous people in the collection industry. Surprise! That's true with every industry, including the medical profession, charities, and the clergy. The question then becomes how to know you're getting paid what is due you.

Remember that you know every loan in your portfolio. You made copies of all the documents so the collection agency cannot hold your papers hostage. You also know the face value of all those loans.

After deciding on a collection agency but before they begin work, you say the following to Russell, your account manager:

> Russ, you know I'm new to the business because I told you that. I do want to be able to monitor your progress because that's really important to me.
>
> The other reason is I want to learn this business. I hope to be buying a lot of loans over time, which will be good for you and for me.

> So I kind of would like to know a little more than maybe some of your other customers do. Would that be a major inconvenience for you?
>
> Hopefully Russell will say "no." If he says "Well, what do you have in mind?," you say:
>
> Well, Russ, on Friday of each week I'd like to get a report on the accounts you've contacted, and the ones you made a settlement on. Would that be something you could do for me?

If he says no or words to that effect, he's going to need an excellent reason. Maybe their system is online, so he doesn't want to fetch a report each Friday. That's fine. But he can hardly justify giving you less than you just asked for.

Once you have that report, I suggest you do a "retroactive audit" periodically. We did it all the time with our account officers.

Your collection agency shows that Roger Maxwell settled for $5,000 three months ago. Great. You call Roger and say:

---

**You:** Hi, Mr. Maxwell, I'm doing a customer survey for Ajax Collections Agency and I see here in the file that you settled your account for $6,000.

*I know the number is $5,000. I have purposely said the wrong number and I'm waiting to see what his response is.*

**Mr. Maxwell:** Um, I think it was $6,500. Hey, Mary, that boat settlement thing was for $6,500, right? Yeah, it was $6,500.

**You:** Well, thank you. I appreciate that. Oh, I see that here, I was just looking on the wrong line of my report. Now, before I hang up, what date do you have on that, Mr. Maxwell? Do you remember when that was?

---

This is where I want to get some specifics, because I seem to have a problem. Roger paid $6,500 and the agency reported only $5,000 to me. We're going to have a little chat with the agency when I get off the phone.

On the other hand, if he says: "Ha ha, not me, man! I only paid three grand!" You say the same thing: "Oh, I see that. I misread the account." Then you say:

> Thank you, and oh, by the way—was the account officer courteous? Was he respectful? He was? Good, would it be a big inconvenience for you to send me a small note? You can just use a ballpoint pen on a Big Chief tablet.

You've now accomplished four things:

1. You're auditing your file to make sure you get all the money that's rightfully yours.
2. You're letting the collection agency know when you are catching discrepancies. They should not play that little game with you in the future—if you even decide to stay with them. That's a judgment call, because everyone makes mistakes.
3. You're finding out how that agency treats your customers.
4. You will grow your testimonial file.

### Evaluating Your Agency

You get your regular Friday report after the agency is up and running with your customers.

You see there are twelve names on it, with what they agreed to in terms of settlements, as well as bankruptcies, deaths, and so on. You know you have 1,200 loans in the portfolio and they talked with twelve of them in one week. You realize this is going to take longer than you anticipated. At least you have a measuring device now.

Now call your contact at the agency and say, "Hey, congratulations on the twelve! Thanks. Good job. Now let's talk about the others. Should I expect this rate to be the normal course of events?"

Maybe he says that it was only a partial week because it was the first week. Maybe he doesn't. You will need to gauge his response in comparison to what you were led to believe during the negotiations.

At any rate, you now have set your standards for them, and you finally have something to measure with. You also can view the report and say:

> Hey, you settled this Maxwell loan for 50 cents. That was really quite a bit better than I had anticipated. Do you have any information on that? What caused him to be so good?

What a great way to learn this business. Just one note of caution: Don't become a pest. If you have two or three thoughtful questions, then great. But let the agency do its job and report the results to you. If you go overboard and burn them out in comparison to the money they're making from you, they'll give you back the accounts.

On the other hand, if they quit demonstrating their capacity to serve your needs, you need to find someone else. Be prepared to terminate quickly if it becomes unproductive. It won't come as a big shock to them because they're only paid on a contingency basis. They won't want to keep working stuff that's not making them any money.

## Settlement Authority

Your collection agency will ask for what level of settlement authority you allow. Though you could insist that they contact you every time they have a customer on the phone who's talking settlement, I would not advise that. It will become too cumbersome.

I suggest that you delegate a specific level of authority. It depends on what you paid for that box, so I cannot give you a firm rule.

You might say that anything over 50 cents on the dollar is acceptable, and they must call you for anything under 50 cents on the dollar. It might be that they have an e-mail process and would like you to respond within 24 hours. That would be fine.

## In the Next Chapter

As I said, none of this is theory. After 4.5 million customers and $15 billion of loans, I can confidently say that we proved what works and what doesn't.

Here's a little secret: To succeed in this business, you don't have to be crafty and you don't even need to be overly intelligent. We deal in common sense. You own the loan and are talking with somebody to whom you can give a big discount. Why should that relationship be adversarial? Why would you ever think it was adversarial?

My money says that if you take action and get into this business, you may very well be hooked. You will not only be helping people, but can become amazingly wealthy at the same time.

Nevertheless, I don't care how good an opportunity is: Smart businesspeople always have an exit door. You may stay in the business for a long time. Then again, you might decide to retire to that tropical island you've had your eye on.

Either way, you should know how to wrap up a loan portfolio. That's the topic of the next chapter.

CHAPTER
9

# How to Dispose of Your Portfolio

**A**ll good portfolios come to an end.

You may decide that it's your last portfolio; on the other hand, you may be hungry for more. Either way, you will reach a point of diminishing returns.

If you're watching your revenues and expenses, at some point you go "upside down." That's when it is not worth your while to spend any more time and money on some loans in your portfolio.

Now what?

## Don't Throw Away—Recycle

What did you do with First National Bank? You walked in and explained that there was value in their basement, in the form of charged-off loans. The bank had reached its own point of diminishing returns. It's just that they didn't know people like you and I were interested in picking up where they left off.

So it is with your portfolio. Don't just shred those loans that even you could not collect from. There may be someone else willing to pick up the cause after you—and pay you for it.

## Come on, Bill: There's nothing left in that box.

All I'm saying is that you should let the marketplace determine that—not you.

On my web site, I list some loan brokers. Go to www.RoadTo MajorWealth.com and type "loan brokers" into the search box. It's not an exhaustive list, so also spend a few minutes on Google, looking for other loan brokers. There's always someone starting out in this business who wants to take a whack at creating value from the stuff other people throw out.

Remember our example of paying 2 percent for those loans at First National Bank? In the business that's called *200 basis points* because 100 basis points equals 1 percent.

Well, I've recently seen portfolios online where the *asking price* was 50 basis points. That means they were starting the negotiations there, and might accept less! Now, these loans were not pretty. Most looked quite old. Still, for an efficient collection operation, it might be profitable to work that portfolio.

Of course, after too long, loans will have gone beyond the state statutes of limitations. Other loans may be in the category of bankruptcy or deceased borrowers. But as long as loans are legally collectible, you should see who might buy them.

## At what point is my portfolio too small?

Again, let the marketplace decide that.

## Consider Other Auction Outlets

You may not realize that companies like eBay will let you list the strangest things. Of course, crazy people have tried to list body parts, their kids, and so on. I'm not talking about that.

The good news is eBay has no problem with people listing their used sneakers, used lipstick, and much more bizarre items: Two sisters from Virginia sold a cornflake in the shape of Illinois for $1,350 on eBay. I kid you not.

If some flake will buy a flake on eBay for $1,350, might you be able to make a good case about selling a portfolio whose face value is impressive?

I'm not suggesting that you mislead anyone about the value. You should require bidders to sign a confidentiality agreement. But there just might be one or more buyers for your wares.

## Three Kinds of Loans

There are only three categories of loans in your portfolio.

### First Type

These are loans that have resolved themselves. It could be a happy ending, where you work out a settlement with the customer. Or it could be a sad ending, where the person declares bankruptcy or dies. Either way, these loans are history.

### Second Type

These are loans that you have put on a payment plan. They may be sending you a nice amount monthly, or maybe only $10 a month until hell freezes over. Such loans are called *set ups* in the business.

You don't have to wait around to collect on that full future stream of checks. You can readily sell that paper to companies that will give you a discounted amount today in cash. Their discount depends on many factors, including how long they'll have to wait for all the checks.

### Third Type

These loans are still technically collectable. You either couldn't collect on them, or chose not to bother.

Here again, you may have some options: You cannot do anything with the first type, but could package up the second type and third type and sell them together. Or you may find separate buyers for the second and third types. It depends on how successful you are at matching portfolios with buyers.

A broker who specializes in set ups may find a customer willing to pay more for that component than if you bundled it with loans of the third type.

Because it does not cost brokers to list your portfolio electronically, they generally are pretty willing to stick it out there and see who bites.

## Preparing Your Loans for Sale

I don't care what industry you're in: If you are a true professional, you have an eye on the eventual sale of an asset when you first get into it. You also take steps while you own the asset to make it as saleable as possible down the road.

In a prior career I owned a lot of real estate. I would typically buy a property from a seller whose records were in shambles. I'd need to work and hunt for what he was paying for utilities, whether there was an environmental hazard on the property, and a hundred other concerns.

If I bought the property, I would not only keep my records in good order, but I'd update them from time to time. I can tell you that when I went to sell that property, I blew away the buyer with how clear and well-organized my property package was.

That translated into more dollars for me: I saved the buyers a lot of time so they could act more quickly. They also could get financing faster because their lender was impressed with the package, too.

People will discount for unknowns. If they are unsure about something, they will offer less than the face value for it. On the other hand, they'll sometimes pay face value or even higher when they're confident and impressed with the item in question.

It's no different in the loan industry. Once you build that spreadsheet on your customers, keep it updated. Maintain the paper files in neat order, and make absolutely sure you—or your collection agency—document all customer contact in detail.

Ask yourself what you wanted to know about this portfolio before you bought it, and make sure the clear answers to those questions are in the package.

Note: When selling through a professional like a broker, don't bother trying to embellish the portfolio or talk it up in some non-factual way. The broker does not care about your opinion. He only cares about the opinion of potential buyers, who will form their own judgment of value. By the same token, don't apologize for what you perceive to be a mediocre portfolio. That's for the buyer to conclude.

## The Sales Process

When you deal with a loan broker, that person will prepare his own confidentiality agreement before dealing with your portfolio. It's the way it is done in the industry.

Don't be surprised, though, if the broker says:

Bill, why don't you write up a summary of what it is you're willing to represent this box of loans to be? You tell me how many, how much, how often, what category described, and I'll send you a little blank form I want you to fill out.

The broker may actually not want to look inside your box. He's thinking: "I don't want to be the one to tell my buyers what's in there. Bartmann's selling it. Bartmann should tell my buyers what's in there. I'm just the intermediary."

In that case, when you make a representation about what's in your box of loans, make sure it's accurate! Do not embellish the facts or it will come back to bite you.

If you prepare your portfolio the way I suggest, you won't need to embellish anything because it will be impressive enough.

Oh, and make sure you don't go cheap and try to save on attorney's fees. Get a good lawyer to represent you in such transactions. Initially it will be a little more expensive, because it's all being arranged for the first time. Later sales should cost you less.

## In the Next Chapter

In other professions you must think long and hard about getting out. It may be difficult to value the business or to find buyers. In the case of the loan industry, you have extreme flexibility. You can be in or out of the business in the way that best suits your lifestyle.

Speaking of lifestyle, that's what it's all about! Though it's nice to help other people to repair their credit and their lives, it's also nice to enjoy the fruits of your labor. That is one of the things I discuss in the next chapter.

# Mental Checkup
# and Reward Time

I t may seem odd, but this may very well be the most important chapter in the entire book.

That's because this chapter is all about what's in your head, and how to optimize it.

The name of the street gang I was in as a teenager was the Manor Boys. There were about 40 of us. We got that name because we took over a big abandoned house, or "manor." Please imagine for a moment what it might be like to put 40 teenage boys together, with no adult supervision and nothing meaningful to do. After all, we were all dropouts.

On a regular basis we broke all of the Ten Commandments. Frequently we broke the law. Most of us were addicted to one or more drugs. None of us joined the priesthood. Many of us soon landed in jail or the morgue.

One kid was tough, but a runt. He wasn't the smoothest-talking member. He certainly was not the strongest or handsomest. And his so-called "education" left him reading at the fifth-grade level.

That sad failure was the one who went on to become a billionaire. So what made me different from all those other more-likely-to-succeed gang members?

I've thought long and hard about that one. I attribute it to my special Bill Bartmann flavor of AA. And I don't mean *Alcoholics Anonymous*.

I'm referring to *Attitude and Action*.

## Attitude Boosters

First, let's talk about ways to boost your attitude.

### *"What If"*

When I was worse-than-broke and owed a million dollars, I saw that ad in the newspaper about a bank that was auctioning bad loans. My initial attitude was "How stupid is that!" But something in me kept coming back to that ad.

As I mentioned before, the billion-dollar attitude happened when I gave myself the latitude to think creatively by using the words "what if." I strung together a whole set of what-if ideas:

- *What if* I could buy those loans cheaply—I mean really cheaply?
- *What if* I could get someone else to finance the loans?
- *What if* I could find a way to be successful on the phone with those borrowers when everyone else could not?
- *What if* I could make enough money to pay off the financing, pay back part of my million-dollar debt, and make a few bucks?

Therefore, Attitude Booster #1 is opening yourself up to possibilities by saying "what if."

## Side-View Mirror

You know that printing on your car's side-view mirror: OBJECTS IN MIRROR ARE CLOSER THAN THEY APPEAR.

Well, the same is true with success. People can convince themselves of just about anything. When your circumstances are in fact bad, it's easy to decide they'll always be bad and you'll never catch a break; the world is full of pain and disappointment, so why should you expect anything different, and so on.

The billion-dollar attitude difference is to realize that *small adjustments can result in major changes*. As a gang member—or as a broke businessman—if I had tried to get my head around all the things I'd have to do in order to become successful, I'd quickly go into overload.

Instead, I focused on making tiny changes in the right direction:

- When I was paralyzed, I simply focused on moving my toes.
- When I began that improbable business of debt collection, I simply focused on the very next phone call I needed to make.

Tiny changes have a way of slipping under the doom-and-gloom radar. You can make them without a lot of planning. Done consistently and over time, they can add up to major improvements in your circumstances.

## Personalize It

My hearing problems prevented me from passing the U.S. Marines physical, so I can't speak about military service from personal experience. But I'm told that a peculiar thing happens to soldiers in wartime.

When they're asked to perform some unbelievably dangerous and frightening act, it turns out that:

- They don't do it for their country, even though they love their country.

- They don't do it for their commanding officer, even though they're fearful of him.
- They don't do it for their family back home, even though they'd do anything for them.

What I'm told is they jump out of that foxhole and become heroes because they're doing it for their buddies. It's that personal connection that creates powerful, instant motivation to defy the odds.

I kept a secret for 25 years. When I was 14 and dating Kathy, her sister Connie told Kathy not to hang around me. She said I was a bad kid. In hindsight, she was absolutely right, but at the time it hurt me.

When I was going to school days and working nights, there were times just about daily when I wanted to hang it all up. But I had posted an index card with Connie's name on it above my desk. Whenever I reared back from my studies and was about to get up, I would see that card and remember her opinion of me. Then I would think of Kathy and sit back down.

*Forbes* magazine interviewed me about my secrets to success, 25 years later. It was only then that I revealed Connie's 10-second comment and what profound leverage I extracted from it.

I'm all for lofty ideals. I have a few myself. I just know that when you need daily motivation, find a positive symbol ("I'm doing it for her") or a negative symbol ("I'll show him!"), and keep it right in front of you.

## It's All about Action

The astronaut Jim Lovell says there are three kinds of people:

1. Those who make things happen
2. Those who watch things happen
3. Those who wonder what happened

I couldn't agree more. There is something magical about action.

First, taking action separates you from easily 80 percent of everyone else. Taking consistent action brings the number up to 98 percent. You think I exaggerate? Consider this:

- They wallow in self-pity—and don't take action.
- They conclude it wouldn't work anyway—and don't take action.
- They don't decide what action to take—and don't take action.
- They wait until just the perfect time—and don't take action.
- They try it once, don't enjoy instant overwhelming success—and don't take action.

Do any of these profiles sound like people you know? Case closed.

## Size Does Not Matter

Don't worry about making big, bold steps. Just worry about taking one step beyond where you are today.

Here's an extremely useful approach: Think about what is the very next actual step you can take on a project. I am not talking about statements like: "Get my first loan portfolio." That's an outcome, not a step. The very next step might be "Finish Bill's book." After that it might be "Look up web sites Bill listed," and so on.

When I say "very next step," I mean it. There must not be anything in the way of that step. For example, if you're stuck on what to say when you first call a borrower, it's no good to list your step as "Figure out what to say." That's what you're stuck on!

You need to break it down into smaller parts you can easily handle. Your next step might be "Sit down and list all the questions and concerns holding me back from making that first call." From that list you might discover a half dozen small steps you can take.

Often inaction is due to lack of clarity. When you work at breaking down those big stone blocks into individual pebbles, they're much less intimidating.

### Someone's Listening to You

I'm a firm believer in the power of your subconscious. Most people don't have the vaguest understanding of the astonishing power of that part of their brain.

In case you doubt having a subconscious in the first place, tell me if this has ever happened to you: You were talking with someone and tried to recall a fact, name, or whatever. For the life of you, the name would not come to you. Then five minutes later, after you had been talking about something else, suddenly you said, "I remember! His name was Gus Monroe!"

You weren't even on the topic of Gus anymore, because you had moved on to another topic. Yet you had sent a command to your subconscious, which quietly worked in the file room of your brain and retrieved that information.

Your subconscious takes your comments *literally*. It is not the reasoning part of your brain. It's the memory and calculation part. Like a massive computer, it does not challenge the commands you type into the keyboard. It simply tries to fulfill them as best it can.

Here's where people sabotage themselves: When they make a mistake, they casually say things like "What an idiot I am!" You might think that's harmless, but it is not. I'm convinced it's a command to your subconscious to not expect more, but to continue the behavior that resulted in the "idiot" comment.

If you're trying to remember something, it's much more productive to say "I'll think of it in a moment," and then move on. Contrast that with people who say destructive things like "Oh, why can't I remember that name! I must be getting old!" That is a really stupid thing to say or even to think.

This is not trivial. It happens with much larger issues. For instance, even the following statement to yourself is counterproductive: "Someday I'll be rich."

Why? Because the literal part of your brain is hearing "Not today, but at some point in the future, I'll be rich."

Here too, you're much better off getting specific. Say "I know I can figure this out, and when I do, I'll be one step closer to my goals." Now that's a statement in the right direction.

Unless you already are a big believer in your subconscious, I bet that you'll notice multiple instances in the next week where your thoughts and self-talk are sabotaging your success. I suggest you clean house and replace them with constructive thoughts.

At first, just strive for simple awareness of these statements. Then as you reliably catch them, you can restate those thoughts in the direction of your success.

### Strategic Reward

Psychologists call it *positive reinforcement.* It's critical to your success. I just finished telling you about how your subconscious mind takes things literally. Well, if you succeed at something—large or small—do not say to yourself: "I could have done that a lot better. I just have to work harder."

Maybe you could indeed have done it better. There will be time to improve later, but if you succeeded in something, then reward yourself. Start small, and work up to the bigger stuff.

What do I mean by "small?" When I was a starving student, Kathy and I had a ritual. We worked hard all week so we could enjoy a night out. By "night out," I mean we treated ourselves to dinner at the local taco joint.

We each got one taco.

If either of us had an especially big week, we'd pull out all the stops and splurge. We bought a third taco and split it.

Therefore, please don't tell me how broke you are, or how you're out of time, or how all your rewards are out of reach. Find something you can look forward to. Then, when you meet some challenge—even if it's just doing the very next step of making a phone call you dread—give yourself a small reward.

You need not take it to extremes and feed yourself figurative dog biscuits for every little thing. Just aim first to eliminate the destructive self-talk. Then aim for always having a reward around the corner. Now you're headed in the right direction.

As an entrepreneur, it is you who is the goose that's laying golden eggs. Perhaps they don't get laid very often right now, and maybe you need a microscope to see them. Whatever. They're gold. You must take good care of that goose and encourage bigger eggs to be produced.

## Turn Around Occasionally

Have you ever hiked in the mountains? Before you start up to that peak, it really doesn't look that daunting. Then as you go up, you discover there's hill after hill. Just when you think you're scaling the last hill, you reach a crest and see more of them ahead.

It's important to turn around and see how far you've come. I'm talking about an affliction that some highly successful people share. They're so focused on their goals that all they see is the mountain looming in front of them. They never turn around to see the progress they've made, not to mention enjoy the view.

Don't hike up your goal mountain for the sake of hiking. It gets back to that fragile "hard work leads to reward" cycle you must reinforce in your brain.

After I had made that first $63,000 from that first $13,000 portfolio of loans, I had a choice. I could do what I did: "Hey, that's pretty cool! It worked! Way to go, Bill. It's Taco Time. Now let's do that again."

Or I could have stated it differently:

> Well, Bill, you've succeeded in holding off the inevitable a bit longer. Yippee, you've paid down your million-dollar debt by $40,000 by busting your butt. Do you seriously think you can duplicate this lucky break 24 more times to repay that million bucks? And if you do—again yippee—you'll still be flat broke.

Dear reader, that's no way to think if you want to go from wherever you are right now and make it to the Big Time.

## Test

Most things in life are not black and white. They're gray areas, open to interpretation. A big hindrance to your Action Engine is when you engage in a lot of speculation. It's easy to say, "That will never work." It's incredibly easy to say, "My situation is different from Bill's—I'm a woman," or "I don't live in Oklahoma," or "I'm in medical school and my parents would kill me if I didn't become a doctor."

The most successful people I know will notice when the excuses, speculation, and reasons not to act begin to kick in, and they stop themselves. They then say three simple words:

"Let's test it."

It's really just a variation on the "what if" secret I gave you earlier. You must suspend Pre-Judgment + Inaction, and replace it with Attitude + Action.

Maybe it won't work. Let's go find out. Maybe it needs adjusting and once you do that, it will work even better than you originally thought. Let's go find out.

## Start before You're Ready

Successful people get used to having a certain number of butterflies permanently living in their gut. They accept a moderate amount of discomfort as part of being successful.

Look at it this way: If the road to real success were a smooth, freshly paved interstate, everyone would be on there.

No, the road to real success is that rocky, winding, hilly path that looks way overgrown with weeds. That's because so few people venture down it.

You must begin before you're ready. I don't mean you should close your eyes and fire blindly in any direction.

Let's say you're at the point that your next action could be to pick up the phone and call your first borrower. You have a major flock of butterflies in your stomach:

Will I be yelled at? Did that Bartmann guy tell me everything I really needed to know about making the call? Do I need to go pay some bills right now, or maybe start dinner? Oh, I know— I'll do some more role-playing on what the call will be like, and I'll do that first thing tomorrow morning.

No, you won't. You're going to sit your butt down in the chair and make that first call. No one is going to come through the telephone line and strangle you where you sit. You'll be fine. Hey, you might even screw up and say the wrong things. Big deal. Then again, you might say the right things, and a check is that much closer to appearing in your mailbox. That truly is a Big Deal.

The important thing is you started before you were totally, completely, 100 percent ready. Why? Because you'll never be that ready, and you'll always be able to gin up some excuse for becoming more ready than you are today.

When you take that next action before being totally ready for it, you have just shown your true spirit of entrepreneurship and success. You have my respect, because I've been there countless times before and I know the feeling.

I once heard about an old, grizzled gunnery sergeant who told brand-new recruits all about the Vietnam War they were about to enter. They were at the grenade range, practicing with live grenades. He asked the recruits, "Who's afraid right now?" Only one guy raised his hand.

Sarge then said, "Okay, the guy who raised his hand is the only one I would trust to be in the foxhole with me. All you other idiots are either too stupid to be afraid, or too dishonest to admit it. Either way it's bad. Let me tell you how to be brave in combat. It's actually very easy. Here's the secret. You'll be so afraid that you will wet your pants. Then you will go and do the job with wet pants."

Now let's put this bad-loan opportunity in perspective: No one will be shooting at you. You'll just be picking up the phone and flapping your lips, and soon you'll be cashing checks.

### Stop in the Middle

Anthony Trollope was a famous English author. He had a habit of writing a certain number of words every single day. One day, he finally reached the end of his book and was happy. But he had not actually written his required number of words for that day—so he started his next book!

That's a great attitude for two reasons: First, he had the discipline to write something every day. He took action daily. Second, he didn't write just when he was inspired, and didn't stop writing when his inspiration ran out.

If you stop a project when you're out of gas, it's much harder to restart it. I suggest you always end the day's efforts in the middle of something, especially if you're on a mini-roll. If you know precisely what is the next action you want to take—and if you've already done a good day's work—then stop before you take that next action.

It will be so much easier to start up again tomorrow. You'll be chomping at the bit to take that next step. By the time you take it, you'll be warmed up and much more into the project than if you started cold.

Don't use this advice as an excuse! Don't procrastinate on me and say, "Oh, I know what I'll do tomorrow, so I'll just wait until then." Instead, only employ this tactic at the end of today's full, successful session.

## Make One Dollar

Your goal in beginning this amazing opportunity that I'm telling you about is to make $1 from it.

That's no typo. I said *one dollar*. Here's what will have happened when you make a dollar from this endeavor:

1. You finished this book and decided to take action.
2. More than "deciding" anything, you actually took action.
3. You located a portfolio of loans, and found the nerve to negotiate a deal.
4. You sat down and made calls to some of those borrowers.
5. At least one person sent you money.

Congratulations! You have truly done the very hardest work of the entire project—the work it takes to follow a new system. You couldn't have produced that one dollar unless you had all the pieces in place.

I know, I know: "Bill, it was a ton of work for a lousy dollar!" There's the negative self-talk happening again.

What you need to say to yourself is: "This actually does produce money. Now let's go produce lots more."

However ugly, time-consuming, and faint it is, you now have laid down the pattern for future success. You have a system. Your main goal should be to improve all the parts of the system:

- Find more deals where that first one came from.
- Become more efficient at picking the best deals and paying the least money.
- Get much better at working with borrowers.

## In the Next Chapter

In the next chapter, we'll talk in much more detail about growing this business as large as you please.

# Get Better to Grow Larger

## The Stages of This Business

As you know, I started this business in a position that's worse than flat broke: I was a million bucks in the hole.

I caught the bug very early and decided to see where I could take the business. As I mentioned before, *Inc.* magazine tracks the "500 Fastest-Growing Companies." We were on the list for four years in a row. The only other company on that list to ever grow as fast and as quickly as we did was Microsoft.

My firm grew to become the dominant player in the collections industry, with relationships at 21 of the top 25 American banks. I therefore know this business at every stage. It's time to share some thoughts about each stage.

### Stage One: Flat-Broke Beginner

Although I respect people who have attained great success, I have extra-special respect for people who are just embarking on a journey they've never taken:

- They are not sure what they're getting themselves into.
- They have nothing to show for their efforts, because the journey has not yet begun.
- They probably have self-doubt, not to mention being surrounded by people who may not support them.
- In the case of the collections industry, they're entering an industry with a very bad reputation.

Yet for some reason they forge ahead. If you are one of them, my hat is off to you.

This is the ultimate "entry-level" business. No matter how destitute you are, you can get started if you have two low-cost assets:

- A willingness to start and keep at it; and
- The power of persuasion.

Even if your pockets are turned inside out, if you can persuade somebody to give you the money to buy a box of loans, you're on your way.

Because you're holding this book, you really are well on your way. Simply follow the steps I've outlined for you and that first box of loans is within your reach.

### Working Your First Box

As you know, it's possible to work that first box of loans when your situation is no better than that of the borrowers whose loans you own. A chair, phone, and notepad is all you really need.

With the steps I've given you in this book, you can farm out the actual collection effort to an agency. Because they work on pure contingency, it's no money out of your pocket.

Once you get a tiny stream of cash, you can begin to improve your situation. The very first purchase my company made was a little $40 used database program to organize our files. It lasted us quite a while before we outgrew it. You don't even have to spend 40 bucks for better systems now, given the fact that Google has a free spreadsheet program online.

We eventually upgraded from our kitchen table to the back room of a trucking company with furniture I bought from Goodwill.

Just remember you're on a noble journey. You will be able to grow quickly once you have just the barest of basics in place.

## Stage Two: Managing Growth

Assuming you like what you see when you're working your first portfolio of loans, you will want to buy more.

I suggest that you exhaust your local market. If your experience is like mine, pretty soon the surrounding banks will not have more charged-off loans in their basement. You will own all of them. The next step is to set up an arrangement where they feed you new charge-offs as they occur.

If you do this right, you create an excellent negotiating position for yourself: Pretty soon the banks may realize that their most cost-effective option is to reduce their own collection staff and give that business to you. Now you're really in the "catbird scat." They need you at least as much as you need them.

It might be on your fourth box or your fourteenth: At some point in this intermediate stage of the business, you stop thinking only about transactions and start thinking about strategy. That's when you should be looking for inexpensive help to take over functions of the business.

Remember that one of the critical functions of the business is the collection effort, and you don't want people with prior experience. Once you've seen for yourself how collections comes down to common-sense respectful treatment of customers, you'll be able to consider hiring account officers.

They could be moms coming in part-time, or college students, or many other types of people. You can delay this phase longer if you find a great third-party collection agency. If you've never really located one you liked, then it may be time to bring the function in-house and keep those dollars.

### Branching Out

I've spent a lot of time in this book on the opportunity closest to home for you—going to your local bank. But I also have described the tremendous opportunities coming as a result of the financial meltdown that began in 2008.

You have no shortage of chances to try out many different types of paper: several varieties of real estate alone, not to mention consumer debt, student loans, credit card debt, commercial debt— the list goes on.

I suggest that you continually build and cultivate your network of loan brokers. They are not only extremely knowledgeable, but they can be your "bird dogs," looking out for good packages. Send these people gift baskets of fancy food during the holidays, and never forget to thank them when they give you a heads-up on a new package. Even if that particular box did not meet your needs, you want the pipeline full, so thank the broker and describe just what you're looking for.

Also try out different types of loans to see what works best for you.

### Overlap Can Be Good

Each portfolio has its own signature revenue curve, which depends on the nature of the loans. For one box, you may see the vast majority of collectable dollars arrive within a short time. On another box, you find many more payment plans where the overall dollars are great, but it will take a while to receive them all.

One of your main functions will be to smooth the revenue streams. Like a master chef, you will blend a little of this and a little of that to create a pleasing overall product. When you started in the business, you might have approached it serially—you completed your first box, then bought the second one, and so on.

I still suggest that you be careful not to let your eyes get too wide too fast in this candy store. Make sure you can retire the debt on your previous portfolios before you move on too soon to others.

Mixing it up can work well when you sell off portfolios, too. Your buyers really don't care that some of the loans you're selling them came from a half-dozen different portfolios you bought over time. If you see that there's particular interest in a given type of loan, you can package all of those type loans in your inventory and sell them.

### Start Small, Grow Fast

This has been a key principle of mine for a long time. Whenever I've been successful in business, I used this approach.

You already know the *start small* part of my philosophy. I challenge anyone to start smaller and more desperate than I was. But here's the secret to the *grow fast* part:

Consciously reinvest every possible penny back into the business.

It's hardly a deep, dark secret. And it's pretty common-sense. Yet why do so few businesspeople follow it? Because it takes discipline. It comes down to this:

- Losers subordinate their future prosperity in favor of current pleasure.
- Winners subordinate their current pleasure in favor of *magnified* future prosperity.

I'm a believer in rewarding myself for a job well done. You know that from the previous chapter. However, the trick is to do that rewarding with as few assets as possible, so you can plow the rest back into the business.

When you create a revenue stream from up-front settlements and payment plans, take the bulk of that money and pay off the current loans as quickly as you can, so you can buy a bigger box of loans. Then lather, rinse, and repeat.

Given my poverty background, it would have been so easy for me to blow my earnings on very expensive toys. Then my company would have rambled along at an okay pace for years. By simply delaying the bulk of my gratification, I was able to buy the very nicest toys on the planet.

That can be you, if you follow my advice.

## Stage Three: Seeing the Future

When you are in stage three, you're becoming a player in this business. You are way beyond worrying about your income. You see, once you are making lots of money, it's coming in far faster than you can spend it. You have all the food you want and drive all the cool cars you want. You probably have a few houses scattered around, and still the money keeps flowing in.

The way really rich people keep score is by their net worth. To blow the top off your business and create a jaw-dropping net worth, you must become very good at three skills:

### Skill Number One: Insist on Systems

I suppose if you are painting the Mona Lisa for a few months, you can just let your creativity run wild.

The collection industry is different: It's an extremely high-volume business. To become extremely good at it, you must system-atize everything. Review the main moving parts of your business:

- Building staff and infrastructure
- Identifying suppliers of loan portfolios
- Analyzing loans
- Financing portfolios
- Collecting on the portfolios

Then ask yourself these questions:

- To what degree have I reduced these functions to step-by-step processes?
- How many of them are written down?

- How many of them have measurements that are tracked daily, weekly, monthly, yearly, and period-over-period?
- To what degree are my measurements *lagging indicators* of what's now history, versus *leading indicators* of what is to come?
- Can I evaluate whether my estimated cash recovery predictions were accurate?
- Can I drill down to the individual customer level to see any degree of detail, and drill up to the enterprise level and turn my data first into information, and then actionable knowledge?

You must strive for repeatability, measurement, and high standards. When you start to achieve those, you become a gravitational force in business: Other companies seek you out because they want to work with the best. You are able to charge more because your quality is higher than the competition's. And because you're a lean, efficiently run company, your profits become, well, obscene.

**Skill Number Two: Delegate**
We all know the concept of delegation. But do you know the Seven Stages of CEO Evolution? They are:

**Stage 1: Phone/mail/design/sell/ship.** When you start your business in humble circumstances, you do everything. You're the CEO, but you hold every other designation too, including Chief Janitorial Officer.

**Stage 2: Supervise Employees.** At last you can begin to have other people take over functions you once did.

**Stage 3: Supervise Managers.** If you want to have a full staff of productive employees, each department needs a quality manager, and you must manage the managers.

**Stage 4: Supervise Executives.** When you're big enough, you will have executives, each of whom is running a substantial organization. You must knit all those units together into a synchronous whole.

**Stage 5: Secure Financing.** In the collection business, financing is the fuel that makes everything possible. You must be on top of the vast flow of funds.

**Stage 6: "Next."** What new product lines, products, and services should the organization be planning today, building tomorrow, and delivering before the competition does?

**Stage 7: Get Close to Employees and Customers.** Financing may be the fuel, but employees and customers are the engine of the business. The happier and more active they are, the more prosperous we all become.

I went through each phase of this evolution. As a millionaire, I spent most of my time in stages 2 to 4. As a billionaire, I spent most of my time in stages 5 to 7.

When I freed up my time and focused on the Big Picture, it afforded me the ability to see the end of the FDIC business before my competitors did. I reacted and became a major player with the RTC.

A few years later, I was able to see the end of the RTC before my competitors could, and I became established in the credit card arena long before they did.

Delegation gave me the luxury of survival. My competitors were not stupid people. In fact, in a number of ways they were more gifted than I am. Yet my insistence on systems and delegation gave me a window into the future, which they didn't see coming.

### Skill Number Three: Act on Opportunity

We've now come full circle to what I discussed at the beginning of this book. We are on the cusp of the most astonishing opportunity this industry has ever seen.

I gave you all the reasons in Chapter 2, so I won't repeat them here; however, I'd like to make an additional point about the opportunity.

It's temporary. I'm not one of those guys who talks in sweeping terms about the dawn of a new age. I'll leave the poetry to someone else. What I see is an extraordinary opportunity for people willing to set aside their doubts and fears, and go all in.

This is an especially rare window because to different degrees, it's open to everyone. You now know how to take advantage of it if you're just starting in the business. But the largest firms would also do well to ride this wave.

The model my firm chose during the last, smaller opportunity with FDIC, RTC, and credit cards was to become extraordinarily efficient. Our costs were so low that we could outbid our competition and still make gigantic profits. We knew we were in this for the long haul, so we pioneered systems that changed the game.

Other big players in the industry adopted a different model, and I'm not talking about the model of "beating up the customer." What some other companies did was simply to make hay while the sun was shining. They recognized the opportunity, too, but did not invest for the future. Their idea was to get in, eat as much as they possibly could, and leave as soon as the business got competitive. It worked for them.

Two remarkably different business philosophies in exactly the same industry at exactly the same time. Both of them were correct models for the respective parties.

No matter where you are in this business, the stars are aligned for you to make extraordinary profits. Are you going to seize the opportunity?

## In the Next Chapter

If the answer is "Yes, Bill, count me in!", you may be wondering where you can get more information on this special industry. The next chapter contains resources you'll want to know about.

# Where to Go from Here

I suppose you might buy another book of mine if I persuaded you that it's necessary in order to really get started in the bad-loan business. Well, it's not. You truly have a blueprint in this book—a plan that can form the basis of a very large fortune for you.

After all, I had no experience whatsoever in this business when I sat down at that file room table in Tulsa and opened that first box of loans. The fact that you have this book from me is more than enough for you to go out there and knock 'em dead.

Several times in this book I have referred to a companion web site. It's www.RoadToMajorWealth.com. Because this book cannot contain all the various resources I've mentioned, you can find the most current versions at that site.

## Bonus Materials

I am grateful that you went to the effort to buy my book, and then took the further effort to read it. As a way of saying thanks, I have a number of bonus materials that are only available to readers of this book. I do not list this bonus package anywhere else on the Internet.

If you would like instant access to those materials, simply go to the same web site as I list above, www.RoadToMajorWealth.com, and type the word "bonus" into the search box.

## Billionaire Business Systems

I believe that every person has a calling. I don't know what yours is, but I know mine: I get great satisfaction from stretching out my hand and helping people to get up.

When I was an attorney working as a public defender, I represented poor people who were being foreclosed on.

When I built CFS, I made my mark on the debt collection industry by treating millions of hardworking people with dignity and respect. We enabled many of them to get a fresh start.

One of my most recent projects is Billionaire Business Systems. At the web site www.BillionaireU.com, you will find comprehensive resources for small business owners. Although it's a relatively new site, I already have recorded dozens of hours of video, broken into separate sections. In each section, I tackle an important business skill or challenge.

Some of those sections directly relate to what I covered in this book. For instance, I talk at some length about how to prepare a business plan, the ins and outs of loan proposals, how to create an advisory board, and many more topics.

I invite you to visit that site and take advantage of that comprehensive resource, from any computer, any time of the day or night.

## Live Events

At this stage in my life, my family and my time are the two highest priorities, in that order.

As a result, I conduct very few live events. Recently, the number has been shrinking as I do more via books and the Internet.

On rare occasions I do hold live sessions where I am the presenter. Some of these sessions are in-depth discussions of how to start and grow a debt-collection business.

It seems that some people are extremely impatient to reach their goals, so they seek me out for personal instruction. Although my time is far too expensive and limited to help such people one-on-one, my sessions give them access to me live, so I can answer all their questions.

If you want more information on such events when they are scheduled in the future, you can visit www.RoadToMajorWealth .com and type in the words "live event."

Again, thank you for reading my book. I look forward to reading about your future success and someday shaking your hand.

Sincerely,

Bill Bartmann

# GLOSSARY

**amortization**

The liquidation of debt through installment payments.

**balloon**

When a lump sum is due at the end of a loan, it is said to have a "balloon" payment.

**bank charter**

The contractual agreements under which a bank operates. The charter may include federal and state laws and regulations, as well as rules established by the bank itself.

**basis point**

One basis point equals one-hundredth of 1 percent. In other words, 100 basis points is the same as 1 percent. When discussing interest rates, it's often handy to say "125 basis points" rather than "one and one-quarter percent."

## CFS

Commercial Financial Services, Inc. This was the company I started at my kitchen table when I was broke and grew to a multibillion-dollar enterprise.

## collateral

An asset of some marketable value. If a borrower defaults on a loan, at some point the lender can sell the collateral to recover some or all of the debt owed.

## due diligence

To perform due diligence means to analyze an investment opportunity.

## FDIC

The Federal Deposit Insurance Company. It is an agency of the federal government, in charge of regulating federally chartered banks as well as some state-chartered ones.

## face value

If you take out a loan for $1,000, the face value of that loan is $1,000.

## mark to market

When a loan or investment is adjusted to reflect current values, it is marked to market.

## non-performing loan

A loan on which the payments are past due by 90 days or more.

## paper

Paper is another term for debt.

**performing loan**

A loan on which payments are current.

**primary collector**

After a financial institution has been unable to collect on a loan, it will send that loan to the primary collector, which is a third-party collection agency.

**RTC**

Resolution Trust Corporation, a federal agency that was active in the late 1980s and early 1990s to handle the disposition of assets within failed savings and loan associations.

**secondary collector**

After a financial institution has been unable to collect on a loan and the primary collector has also been unable to collect on it, the lender may send the loan to the secondary collector.

**secured debt**

Debt that is backed by collateral.

**subprime mortgage**

A mortgage that is given to a borrower who has significantly less than perfect credit.

**TARP**

Troubled Asset Resolution Program. It was created in late 2008 to deal with the "rescue" or bailout of failing financial institutions.

**tertiary collector**

In some cases, multiple parties have been unsuccessful at collecting on a loan, including the financial institution, primary collector, and secondary collector. The tertiary collector is the third independent collection agency hired to try to collect on the loan.

**thrifts**

Another name for savings and loan associations.

**unsecured debt**

Debt that is not backed by any collateral.

# INDEX